PERSPECTIVES ON DEATH AND DYING Series

DEATH, DYING, TRANSCENDING

EDITED BY
RICHARD A. KALISH

Ⴆ Baywood Publishing Company, Inc.

Library of Congress Catalog Card Number: 78-67779

ISBN Number: 0-89503-011-X

Library of Congress Cataloging in Publication Data
Main entry under title:

Death, Dying, Transcending

   (Perspectives on death in human experience series; 3)
   Includes bibliographical references.
   1. Death — Psychological aspects. 2. Death — Social aspects.
I. Kalish, Richard A. II. Series.
BF789.D4S6 1979   155.9'37   78-67779
ISBN 0-89503-011-X

Preface

Part of being human is knowing that you will die. As far as we know, other animals do not share this knowledge, which adds to our creativity and excitement and exploration . . . and our anxiety and resentment and unhappiness and despair. Those who die too soon feel cheated of the duration of life to which they were entitled; those who die long after their powers have waned may feel cheated of an appropriate death. This is because they know what death is (or at least they have their ideas), and they have a sense of when death is entitled to take them.

Death touches the life of every one of us, not just once but innumerable times. And the touch is not always gentle. Each of us must suffer the loss of others whom we love, and often the suffering is greater in anticipation of the loss than for the loss itself. Each of us recognizes that death forms a boundary to our own lives, and again the concerns are often greater in anticipating that boundary than when the boundary is just a moment away. And each of us contends with our beliefs, desires, fantasies, fears, and expectations of what occurs after death: is the boundary between life and death a boundary between something and nothing? Or is it a boundary between something and something different?

When people contemplate the dying process, they often respond to thoughts of pain, discomfort, loss of control, separation from loved ones, but these experiences also occur to people who are not dying. The unique characteristic of *dying* is that it eventuates in *death*. And death means total cessation of all experiencing. Thus, one of the fearsome qualities of dying is the recognition that all experiencing will some day, perhaps soon, cease.

For some people, of course, death is not the end of experiencing, but a rite of passage to another kind of experiencing. Existence is continuous, although the existence may be manifest in a different physical or psychological or social form.

Death has other kinds of meanings than those of extinction, boundary, or passage. Some people perceive it as a punishment for the sins of the individual; others view death as the price we all pay for the sins of Adam and Eve or for the sins of all humanity. However, death is simultaneously seen as a reward, as the opportunity to gain peace and — for some — a sense of relatedness to a transcendent being. Death is also an organizer of time: just consider how you would spend your time, your hours and your years, if you knew that you would never die. Death requires that you make choices, develop priorities, since there is not enough time to do everything.

iii

And death is loss: loss of meaning, loss of control, loss of plans and projects, loss of body, loss eventually of self. These losses make dying so difficult, because the losses occur during the dying process and loss is fully realized by the moment of death.

One philosopher commented that it is easier to look at the sun than at death. Perhaps so. Perhaps, just as we protect our eyes from the sun, we need to find some way to protect our thoughts and feelings from death. But we still look at the sun and try to understand it, find ourselves enjoying its warmth, realizing that without the sun we would be totally different creatures . . . or not be at all. The sun can destroy us, but it also benefits us. We acknowledge both its destructive powers and its healing powers. I believe we can do the same with death.

Table of Contents

PART 1
The Dying Process

The dying process is deeply personal, yet is also a social phenomenon. It is totally individualistic, yet is shared, and generalizations can be made about it. This section attempts to develop both the personal and the social sides of the dying process.

The section begins with a descriptive and speculative chapter that examines the dying process and the dying person, with a focus on the individual and his or her personal needs. The section then moves on to an attempt to integrate many threads in the weave of dying so that a pattern emerges, a chapter that sketches in a theory of death that is less a theory than an overview of some of the most salient issues, yet tying it all together through role theory.

After the broad strokes of the Kalish chapter, the section looks more closely at two major issues in the care of the dying person: first, the process of communication with the dying, with both the spoken and unspoken messages receiving equal attention, and second, the extent to which discernable stages occur during the dying process. The Schulz and Aderman chapters, a very critical look at stage theory, is likely to be controversial, since it questions a concept that is already so taken for granted that it has invaded introductory textbooks; the Erickson and Hyerstay material is also controversial, but for very different reasons, since it is a sharp attack on some care issues that are often not recognized.

The final two chapters shift the focus considerably. The first of these is a moving personal account by a woman whose husband is dying. As Ms. Paulay's experiences unfold, they generate tension and distress, the more so because the reader can surmise the ending, while the teller of the story cannot, a circumstance that adds more poignancy to the already-poignant chronicles.

The final chapter is a fairly technical research study, selected because it is such an excellent example of research in the service of human needs. Those of you with statistical background will have no trouble with this material, but most of you are probably not familiar with factor analysis or regression equations. No matter. You still know what a factor is, and you can still understand what Weisman and Worden mean by Survival Quotient. The richness of this article is what the research shows, not the statistical manipulations, yet statistics still form the base for its findings.

I've attempted to bring together a range of superior materials focussed around the dying person, ranging from theory to description to research to personal experience. In the next section are articles on the meaning of death.

CHAPTER
1

SO?

Ronald Koenig

At some untimed moment
No different than another
I will gather up my death,
Poof!
Monuments are for mourners.

Then, all of the choices I have made
Against myself,
Will matter now and yesterday
And for — myself,
Will matter not at all

When I awoke this morning
I noticed, unsurprised,
That I had forfeited yesterday to time
And only I could even count it
In the cumulative nature of death.

CHAPTER
2

The Onset of
the Dying Process

Richard A. Kalish

"LIVING is dying." "To be born is to begin to die." "Each time I breathe, I die a little." These statements, in spite of undeniable philosophic implications, are too often used as equivocations when we try to learn more about the actual process of dying. Yet they point up the difficulty in defining the onset of dying. Dwight Eisenhower died after a series of heart attacks dating back to his first term as president; Adlai Stevenson dropped on the street and died soon after; Robert Kennedy was shot and died in a matter of hours. We could, assuming sufficient medical information, plot what Glaser and Strauss (1968) have termed the dying trajectory for each of these men. But we must learn more than the objectively charted trajectory of dying. We must also consider the trajectory as seen by the person himself and by each important person in his environment.

Many people have some form of professional contact with the dying person: one administers to his medical needs, another is concerned with his social and psychological needs, a third applies himself to satisfying his religious needs, and perhaps a fourth is more interested in studying his needs so that the insights can be communicated to appropriate practitioners.

Also, each enters the picture at a different stage. We may enter before or after we are aware that the person is terminal; we may enter before or after *he* is aware that he is terminal. We may enter shortly before death, to administer the last rites, to meet the ambulance in the emergency ward, to comfort those about to become bereaved. We may enter long before the death, as a psychotherapist, a personal physician, or a minister. In each of these situations, the professional sees the dying process through his own eyes. But even professionals often lack information on the dying process as seen through the eyes of the person who is dying.

I would like to discuss first, the process of learning that dying is the outcome of a condition that is already under way; second, the tasks that the dying person must accomplish.

LEARNING OF DYING

Some people never learn that they are dying. They are homicide or accident victims; they die from an initial massive coronary; they die from a progressive disease that has been misdiagnosed, or they have been sufficiently sheltered from knowledge of their real conditions so that death is not anticipated. We can only estimate how many die in this fashion. More and more evidence has accumulated to suggest that the dying person is much more likely to be aware that he is dying than we have previously believed. However, the dying person is frequently unwilling or unable to share his knowledge with others, even though he recognizes that the others have access to the same knowledge. Again referring to Glaser and Strauss (1965), there is a mutual pretense situation.

Most often the fatally ill person has some recognition of his circumstances. To gain this awareness, there must be some sort of informational input. Such input may be categorized in several ways.

First, it may be explicit in varying degrees. The physician who informs his patient point blank of a terminal condition is providing highly explicit information. Data, however, indicate that relatively few physicians will take this frontal approach. More commonly only hints are given. In many instances, the physician conspires with a family member, while the dying person himself is told nothing; nonetheless, he learns—from overhearing conversations, from comparing symptoms to those of people he has known, from the bedside stage whispers of physicians, nurses, relatives, friends, and others, from worried looks on faces, from questions about wills and funerals. The clues are too numerous to mention. One dying woman went so far as to tell her son, her one confidant , that "Everyone must think I'm either stupid or deaf—they stand at the foot of the bed and talk about when I'm going to die, then they come up to the head of the bed and smile and tell me how well I'm looking and how quickly I'll be out of here." Since explicit information is frequently lacking, the terminal person must put together the available information like a puzzle.

Second, the input may be complete or incomplete. There might be the kind of information that permits the person to know, without doubt, that his condition is fatal. Or there might be enough to make a judgment, but without knowing for sure. Completeness and explicitness are related, but are far from identical. A physician might very explicitly tell a patient that his condition is serious, but not give enough information for the patient to determine whether the illness is fatal. An explicit but incomplete statement might be "You have a malignant turmor in your stomach, but it is possible that an operation would remove it." An example of a non-explicit and incomplete statement would be "You seem to have something seriously wrong with you, but we'll do some more tests and see if it isn't something we can take care of." Explicit and complete: "Your tests show that you have a malignancy that is—as far as I can now determine—inoperable." By definition, a complete but non-explicit statement would be impossible. However, the patient may obtain complete information without ever hearing an explicit statement, merely by putting together a variety of vague comments, behavioral nuances, and other clues into a coherent picture.

A third way of categorizing informational input is according to the source of information. The patient may learn from any one or combination of the following ways:

(1) *A direct statement from the physician.* Inevitably, this may occur in a variety of ways, ranging from gentle to abrupt, from lengthy to brief, from encouraging questions and other responses to shutting off discussion;

(2) *Overhearing comments made by the physician to others*. Patients are frequently discussed in their presence as though they were inanimate objects. Stage whispers at the foot of the bed, explanations from physician to nurses, and so forth;

(3) *Direct statements from other health care personnel, particularly nurses*. This would normally occur only in response to direct questioning on the part of the patient, although occasionally a nurse will feel that the physician has shirked his responsibility and she will find some method of eliciting the direct question so that she must answer it. This is a rare circumstance, however;

(4) *Overheard comments made by other health care personnel*. This parallels the statements of physicians;

(5) *Direct statements by others involved, such as a family member, a social worker, a clergyman, or the family lawyer*. This occurrence is also unusual, since for a variety of reasons the physician is normally the individual to take the responsibility for direct comments;

(6) *Overheard comments by others involved*. Again, this is similar to comments overheard from the physician;

(7) *Changes in behavior of others*. In some instances, the visits of the attending physician drop off after a terminal diagnosis is made. The interactions with nurses and other staff members become more abrupt. Friends and relatives who visit may exhibit additional strain through unduly forced cheerfulness, through sudden wires and telephone calls to out-of-town family who soon appear on the scene (after all, what would prompt a brother living 2000 miles away to drop by for a casual visit?), through badly masked tears, through tense admonitions that everything will be all right. Hushed voices or false joviality become more frequent, from both family and professional staff. And, of course, the behavior of the clergyman may show sudden and significant change;

(8) *Changes in medical care procedures*. Different medication is now given. Exploratory surgery produces neither report nor follow-up. The patient is given narcotics and other pain-killers more readily;

(9) *Changes in physical placement*. The patient is moved to another room or another ward. He is sent home or there is talk of sending him home. The physical location has great significance in terms of the progress of his illness;

(10) *Self-diagnosis*. Many patients learn a great deal about their own conditions and the conditions of others. Mixed in with confusion, ignorance, and distortion is a fair amount of truth. Through reading magazine and newspaper articles, through a careful search at the local library, through listening to the fatal symptoms of others, a reasonably valid self-diagnosis can often be made. Even if the diagnosis is incorrect, the degree to which the person accepts it and acts accordingly is extremely important. On several occasions, when my children have shown a particular symptom, I have gone to my wife's old pediatric nursing books to make certain that the symptoms were associated with relatively harmless illnesses. Sick people will frequently find such a source of information describing their own symptoms. One close friend of ours had just finished reading a *Newsweek* article that described her symptoms so accurately that only her own incredulity prevented an accurate self-diagnosis on the spot;

(11) *The signals from within the body*. As pain and discomfort increase, as curative and ameliorative efforts become progressively less successful, as sedation becomes more necessary, the fatally ill person often senses the changes within his own body and recognizes that his future is brief. Again, he may be totally wrong, but we are now concerned with subjective reality, not medical reality;

(12) *Altered responses to personal futurity*. Discussion of the future suddenly takes a new tack. Visitors and hospital staff become reluctant to talk about future plans. Queries about funerals, burial, wills, and so forth enter the conversation surreptitiously—or else are aggressively avoided. Slips of the tongue are made and corrected with great embarrassment.

The response of the dying person to these clues is a joint function of (1) the clues themselves, (2) himself as a person, i.e., his background, religious beliefs, personality structure, cognitive and sensorimotor capacities, etcetera, (3) his present life status, i.e., medical condition, age, financial status, etcetera and (4) the circumstances causing his death. Patient A learns of his coming death by overhearing a conversation between his physician and the floor nurse; the diagnosis is a broken hip complicated by pneumonia; he lives alone, does not attend church or have strong religious beliefs, has no performance decrement, and is a mild and passive person. Patient B is told of his condition by his physician while his wife is with him; he has suffered a series of increasingly serious strokes and is expected to receive another; he lives with his family, attends the Catholic church, has major psychomotor impairment but no cognitive change, and hates the idea of being dependent or inactive. Patient C has almost succeeded in a sincere suicide attempt; he overhears the ambulance driver telling the physician on duty in the emergency room that his respiration rate suggests a very high risk of death or permanent cognitive impairment; he is a depressed, self-deprecating person who has attended the Methodist church on occasion. Patient D's family and physician have done an excellent job of keeping her condition from her. Unfortunately they ignored the fact that Mrs. D.'s mother died of a similar form of cancer, and Mrs. D. diagnosed herself long before the physician was certain enough of the diagnosis to inform the family. Mrs. D. is a self-sacrificing person whose life has revolved around her family and her ability to protect them from any harshness.

These thumbnail sketches should suggest quite different responses to the informational input. As we learn more about each of the variables and their relationship to patient response, we can begin to make predictions about what the patient will do. To take a relatively simple example: assume that the physician has informed the patient directly, that the patient is a stable and emotionally healthy person, that he is elderly with no dependent survivors, that his condition indicates a relatively painless death—we could predict an effective coping response. I've obviously loaded the dice—most people are not so ideal.

A person can respond to the informational input in many ways. He may be able to absorb the information immediately and completely, even though it is totally unexpected. Or he may accept one clue, live with it a while, and learn to deal with the entering wedge of probability of impending death, then return to consider another clue. Or he may vacillate, move back and forth between acceptance and denial, or both accepting and denying simultaneously. He may overtly express his knowledge that he will die, while not emotionally accepting it. Conversely, he may be able to accept his own dying, but be unwilling to verbalize his feelings and knowledge. And he may deny his circumstances completely. Many physicians have reported making a direct, explicit statement to a patient concerning his medical condition, only to have the patient deny ever having heard such a statement a month later. The patient, of course, can distort the information by seizing upon the thread of hope the physician holds out, by seeking other medical opinions or treatment, by visiting faith healers and others who offer pseudo-medical help, by redefining the probability of survival, by denying the existence of a particular symptom, and in other ways.

Each of the situations described above can be plotted on a subjective trajectory. The subjective trajectory of the person who learns, without prior hints, that he will die shortly and who accepts the information, would be a straight line function from upper left to lower right. For others, the trajectory will dip and jump up, will blur and become indistinct, will bounce rapidly up and down like a kymograph measuring a rapid heartbeat.

Plotting the subjective trajectory next to the objective trajectory would also have value. To what extent does the intellectual awareness and emotional acceptance of the fatally ill person parallel his dying process? To what extent might the subjective trajectory exert force upon the objective trajectory, i.e. to what extent does one's belief about his own survival possibilities influence the actual survival possiblities? The subjective trajectory may never reach the point of dying, regardless of the path of the objective trajectory. Conversely, the subjective trajectory, due to misinterpretation of non-explicit and incomplete input, may move to the point of dying, when the patient's medical condition is still reversible.

To translate the latter comment from jargonese to English: the patient may misinterpret clues and assume he is dying, when in actual fact he is not at all likely to die. In this context also, the family mutual pretense situation will prevent the patient from establishing an effective two-way communication system. He does not know how—or is unwilling—to send out the kind of signal that would elicit the feedback needed to give him appropriate answers. Knowing that the dying person is not told the truth (indeed, he has probably participated in the deception of others), the non-dying patient may ignore all the clues that tell him he is healthy and will recover, but will attend primarily to those clues that may be interpreted as suggesting a fatal illness. After all, it is very easy to re-interpret a sincere smile into a forced smile, a valid word of encouragement into an attempt to reduce anxieties, a conversation between doctor and nurse as to the outcome of the football pool into a conversation on a forthcoming rapid decline.

For the dying person—and equally for the person who suspects that he is dying—vague and otherwise meaningless events suddenly become Rorschach cards into which he projects his fears and hopes. If the psychological set is that dying is likely, the interpretation of the environment will reinforce the set. The more his circumstances, his past history, his symptoms, etcetera resemble his concept of a fatal illness, the more likely he is to interpret whatever feedback occurs as signifying dying.

TASKS OF THE DYING PERSON

As the fatally ill person copes with the process of learning about his own coming death, he also undertakes a variety of added tasks. Until his acceptance of his own fatal condition is complete, his need to accomplish the related tasks may not be sufficient to produce action or at least to produce sustained action. As an example: a dying person might need to consider the financial circumstances of his survivors and plan for them. However, a non-dying person either is required to make other plans or is able to postpone the entire concern of planning. As the ill person is increasingly convinced that he is dying, he may be increasingly motivated (assuming physical and intellectual functioning is appropriate) to plan for the family. Very possibly he will pass through periods when dying seems impossible or improbable. At any given point in time, denial may be struggling with reality so that he simultaneously feels that he (a) must and (b) need not take immediate steps in this regard.

This may serve as the first example of a task of the dying person: he must contemplate arranging a variety of affairs. Inevitably he does not have to do anything concrete—but it is doubtful if he can avoid contemplation. Thus, he may wish to verify, alter, or initiate a will; he wants to have back debts paid off; he may have messages for friends, neighbors, relatives, co-workers. He wants to discuss funerals, burial, autopsy, tissue donation. As I write this, I am asking myself what I would wish to arrange if I had just learned I would be dead within six months. I would need to make arrangements for students, grades, exams, etcetera. I would see to it that a brief codicil was added to my will. I would make explicit my desire for cremation. I would try to pull together my insurance policies to make sure none of them would expire before me. I would talk to an insurance agent or other adviser about how much money my family would need to live on and how we could come closest to arranging for it. I would suggest to what institution I wished to donate my books and journals. There are undoubtedly other arrangements, including, of course, those that involve inter-personal relationships.

My previous comments presuppose, of course, that I am sufficiently intact mentally and physically to make the arrangements. Often pain and discomfort, fear and anxiety, or confusion and disability prevent the dying person from taking such a direct role in arranging his affairs. Of course, if denial has caused his personal trajectory to reject the possibility of dying in spite of his medical trajectory, he may refuse to make such arrangements because he would feel they were unnecessary.

In addition, if the dying person has received misleading input, he may make inappropriate decisions. Often the family is able to take over most decision-

---

*For a totally different approach, see the excellent book *On Death and Dying* by Elizabeth Kuber-Ross, Macmillan, 1963.

making functions (and therein is a topic worthy of a paper on its own), while the ill person merely signs the papers. However, why should a sick person, intellectually intact and led to believe that his condition is reversible, suddenly add a codicil to his will, bring together his life insurance policies, and decide whether he wants to donate his eyes to an eye bank.

What occurs is obvious: either the person receives enough input to provide a reasonably clear picture of what is taking place, or else some tasks may be left undone. A mutual pretense situation does not permit the freedom to discuss the dying process, and those in his environment are unable or unwilling to provide the required information. In order to arrange his affairs properly, the dying person must have a reasonably accurate perception of his trajectory, i.e. his personal trajectory should not deviate too far from his medical trajectory. This means that three things must have occurred: first, he must have received sufficiently explicit information, or have been able to bring together information from various sources into an explicit understanding, so that he can recognize the extent of his potential for death; second, he must have received sufficiently complete information to enable him to be fully aware of his condition; third, he must be psychologically able to deal with the clues he receives without resorting to extreme denial or repression or other mechanisms that would permit him to turn aside the implications of the informational input.

The second task is that of dealing with loss, both the loss of the survivors and the loss of the dying person himself. The dying person is often deeply concerned with what his death will mean to his survivors in ways other than legal and financial. He will frequently consider their feelings, their grief, their vulnerability, their isolation, their coming need to establish replacement relationships. Mutual pretense prevents any discussion of these feelings; open awareness permits such discussion, at least in some instances. One woman commented that during her last year of marriage, when her husband was terminal, the mutual deceit placed so much stress on top of an already stressful situation that the year was robbed of the potential it did have for closeness and intimacy.

Similarly, the dying person must accommodate himself to his own loss, i.e. that he is going to lose the entire world that he has known and—at least temporarily—all the people in it. Dealing with impending loss, widely discussed in the literature, is one of the most difficult tasks for the dying person. In the final analysis, his tears are probably a combination of his own personal sorrow and his capacity to empathize with the sorrow of others.

Has he been able to help his family find new relationships quickly or has he left them so effectively tied to his memory that they cannot move away? This becomes an interesting value question: who is better (or better off)—the woman whose husband leaves her such rich memories and emotional ties that she never feels the need to remarry or the woman whose marriage relationship was directed at self-fulfillment in such a way that she was quickly able to find a subsequent happy marriage? Which of these two women is paying the greater tribute to her husband?

Task number three is arranging for future medical and other care needs. Often this task can be left to others, but the fatally ill person may wish to take a more active role in the way in which he dies than is presently permitted. He may wish to consider alternate care arrangements: nursing home versus own home versus hospital, hiring a nurse versus utilizing family members, using narcotics or other pain-killers versus retaining as much self-awareness as possible. It is not that the individual need make final decisions, but that he may wish to participate in the decision-making process.

The fourth task is that of planning his future and allocating whatever time and energy (and financial) resources are available. Once again, it is not that each dying person should have a time-energy-money budget that he makes out the first of each month and tabulates on the thirty-first. Rather, the knowledge that death is imminent changes the meaning of time and futurity. The proper allocation of these resources becomes both more important and less important. Is this the time to take a trip? To go on an orgy of eating and drinking and other hedonistic activities or on an orgy of reading and listening to music? Are walks in the woods more important? Is there one final beau geste to be made? Does he want to give away his money while still alive, so that he sees it being enjoyed?

Fifth, the fatally ill person might have to anticipate future pain and discomfort. Additionally, he might be faced with various forms of motor, sensory, and cognitive decrements in performance. Neither of these are pleasant, and, fortunately, most terminal patients can avoid severe physical pain and extensive changes in functional effectiveness. Again, the realities of the situation are less important than the anticipations and the anxieties. We have little accurate (or even inaccurate) information on what the dying person fears in his impending death; we do not know to what extent fear of loss of faculties is felt; we know that fear of future pain is common, but we don't know how common. More important we don't know how to communicate with the dying person to reduce his fears. Suggestions range from LSD to psychotherapy to "never telling the patient the truth because then he will give up hope."

The fear of loss of performance capability is extremely great also. The reaction of horror many people express upon seeing an elderly relative or friend reduced to a semi-coherent, shuffling, forgetful figure is common. "I would rather be dead than end up that way" is a frequent statement. Yet, by the time the condition is far enough advanced to be serious, the person is no longer capable of influencing his own destiny.

Other physical changes can occur with equally disruptive effects. Fatal illnesses often produce changes in appearance that are very difficult for either the sick person or those in his environment to accept. Similarly, unpleasant odors can also occur. Accident victims and burn victims are particularly dramatic examples, but cancer and other diseases can have similar impact.

The loss of physical function, the fear of regression, the recognition of loss of control over physical and cognitive capacities, the coming destruction of the body, all these suggest a loss of self or a loss of identity. If the body is shortly to exist no longer, who is he? (Or, more cogently, who are *you* when your body ceases to function?) Is it sufficient to be a name in the record books, a memory among your friends, a statistic in the Bureau of the Census? The Western concepts of immortality do not require that the physical body be present in corporeal form, but we associate ourselves so completely with our physical body that it is difficult to conceptualize our existence apart from the body.

The sixth task is closely related to the fifth: the dying person needs to cope effectively with his own death encounter. I have already mentioned that he must contend with his feelings of loss. Similarly, he must account for his fear of a *rite de passage* from which no one has returned with descriptions of the demands of the new role; he has to deal with the possibility of permanent extinction; he must consider becoming a non-person, a forgotten person, a person whose continuation resides only in memories, official documents, and a few temporary results of work and human relationships.

Coping with a death encounter inevitably brings up concern with immortality. Some people accept the traditional Christian immortality of abiding with God and Jesus in some self-aware state (with or without a physical body). Others look to living in memories, through artistic or industrial productivity, through children, or other accomplishments as sources of immortality. Whatever the beliefs along these lines, the imminence of death will usually elicit consideration of immortality.

Seventh, the dying person faces the task of making a decision: to the extent that it is in his power, should he attempt to slow down or to speed up the dying process. The will-to-live is far from established as an effective determinant of life and health; yet, in spite of the inadequacy of research literature, clinical literature and personal reports are filled with examples of the importance of the will-to-live. But the patient's attitude extends beyond the will-to-live. It affects his willingness to follow medical orders, to take medication, to restrict certain eating or drinking or smoking or other activities. It is doubtful whether many patients state to themselves that they want to die sooner or later than the physician has predicted and then set about doing something about it. However, the speeding up or slowing down of the dying process is undoubtedly part of a pervasive pattern of response to the entire sickness—dying role.

The last task to be discussed consists of dealing with the numerous psychosocial problems that might beset a dying person. For example, our society condemns dependency, but the dying person must often anticipate a future of increasing dependency. He is going to be a burden upon his family, regardless of whether he wants to or whether his family accepts him willingly. He may need financial help, personal care, housing, and emotional support. The dying person frequently loses mastery over his environment and, thereby, loses one of the major supports of an adequate self-concept. He must make some adjustment to the sick role or the dying role. In so doing, he must accept the idea that others are going to do for him many things that his own selfhood required he do for himself.

A related matter: our society rewards the person who contributes to it, but causes to feel guilty the person who extracts from it. The dying person, with few exceptions, is not going to make any additional contribution to the community or to his family and friends. He will only remove resources from the society. His lack of productivity may be distressing to himself, and he is likely to reject himself to some degree because of it.

THE ROLE OF THE PROFESSIONAL

Much writing and discussion have taken place regarding the needs and the rights of the dying person to learn of his own circumstances. There is little doubt in my mind that the informational input should be as explicit and as complete as the patient is able to accept, that the source of the information should be the physician or someone (family member, friend, minister, or nurse) delegated by him, and that the information provided should err on the side of being too explicit and too complete, rather than insufficiently explicit and complete. Thus, the present tendency is to state "The patient should be informed of his condition if it seems probable that he is emotionally stable and if there is evidence that such information would not rob him of hope." I would suggest the focus be as follows: "The patient should be informed of his condition unless it seems probable that he is emotionally unstable and unless there is good evidence that such information would rob him of hope *and* that such hope is more important than the benefits of an open awareness situation." Shifting the burden of proof would make an immense change in what actually takes place.

When the professional faces the needs of the dying person to accomplish the handful of tasks previously described, the problem becomes more difficult. Let me return to those tasks in this context.

First: Making arrangements, particularly financial arrangements. Someone is likely to have to help the dying person do this. One of the most persuasive reasons for an open awareness context is to enable the individual to realize the urgency that he make necessary arrangements. We may under-estimate the importance, particularly to middle-aged persons, of tying up the loose ends, of arranging for family finances, of feeling assured that things are in order and that the survivors will be able to carry on without him. This offers the dying person mastery over himself and over a portion of his phenomenal field, at least for the time being. It is his arrangements that will be executed, not those of subsequent advisers.

But it is just this time that people are least likely to discuss such matters openly. Fear of being seen as greedy or insensitive may impede such discussion. It is probably better for the subject to be opened by a person not closely involved with the family, e.g. the physician, the social worker, the minister. I can say about this task, as about all others: we need to learn much more about *how* important it is for *which* dying persons.

Second: Arranging for non-financial concerns of survivors and dealing with personal loss. In being effectively humanistic, we need to learn a lot more about how to help the dying person and his survivors to cope with the loss, both when impending and when past history. However, it is not necessary to wait for additional research in order to put into effect what we already know. Nursing school curricula are beginning to include materials on helping patients deal with loss. Medical, social work, and clinical psychology programs are lagging behind. Strangely enough, even the ministers, who have for centuries been the guardians of the gates to existence after death, seem to say little in their training programs regarding the dying or the bereaved.

Three: Arranging for future medical and other care needs. Here again we need to learn about *what* kinds of decisions *what* kinds of patients can make with *what* kinds of effectiveness. It is his death—he should have as much to say about it as possible, even if it distresses the family, irritates the physician, and inconveniences the charge nurse. When a person is terminal, we are inclined to read him off as a non-person and do our planning in terms of those he leaves behind. It is his life as long as he has it, and it is his body after his earthly existence ceases.

Fourth: Allocating time, energy, and financial resources. Dr. Avery Weisman advocates that professionals working with the dying focus upon the time and opportunities that remain, rather than upon those that are lost. What can be done in such limited time? What can be done with a given organic condition? Planning for the future is part and parcel of middle-class America: just because the future is sharply reduced does not mean that planning should cease. Here is an area where all professionals can be helpful, if to do nothing more than help family members help the patient. Dr. Weisman commented that if a person dying of cancer has a hangnail that is getting better, concentrate on the hangnail. To attempt to bring this idea home more forcefully: everyone of us is going to die so that any medical condition we alleviate merely postpones the inevitable day. Therefore, you might contend that it is useless to worry about any painful hangnails you ever may have because you will eventually die. The only difference between you and the patient dying of lung cancer is that there is a very high statistical probability that you will outlive him. The probability is not, however, 1.00.

We all have a future, no matter how brief or how bleak. That future deserves attention. To draw another analogy: at what point do you stop repairing your house? A week before you expect to sell it? A month? A year? A decade? You will never be in that house permanently, so you might argue that any improvement is temporary and should not be worth bothering with. Now change your set and assume that this is the last house you will ever live in—now how do you feel about it? Your decisions probably waver—you are no longer so certain. Perhaps this will help you empathize with the dying person.

Fifth: Anticipation of future pain and performance decrement. As mentioned before, we should try to learn how important this is and to whom. Professionals can do a great deal to help in this regard. Sometimes the dissemination of accurate information is sufficient. In other instances, a good listener to attend to expressions of fear of pain is requisite.

Sixth: Dealing with the death encounter. The task here is similar to that outlined briefly above, except that the task may be more complex and difficult, partly because of the feelings of the professional.

Seventh: The decision to affect the rate of decline. The complexities of this concern are too great to deal with here.

Eighth: Psychosocial problems, including loss of independence, loss of mastery, and loss of productive roles. What does the dying person really fear he will miss most? Diggory and Rothman (1961) investigated seven consequences of one's own death, including (1) inability to have experiences, (2) uncertainty regarding after-life, (3) fear of what will happen to the body after death, (4) concern for survivors, in terms of caring for them, (5) concern for survivors in terms of their grief, (6) ending of plans and projects, and (7) pain. These authors began the investigation, but it has never been followed up. I think they omitted several important consequences. If we can learn what types of role change and capacity change are really the most destructive to the dying person, we might be able to structure his environment to make these losses less important. Again, we do not need to wait for more research before beginning—we have ample information to launch our efforts.

Pattison (1969) discusses the need to respond to the crisis or crises faced by the dying. "Here lies our opportunity to intervene, for although we cannot deal with the ultimate problem of death, we can help the person to deal with the various parts of the process of dying. By focussing on these part-problems, the dying person can cope with himself and with his dying, to some measure, to resolve the crisis in a rewarding fashion that enhances his self-esteem, dignity, and integrity. The dying person can take pride then in having faced his crisis of dying with hope and courage and come away having dealt successfully with the crisis. One might call this healthy dying!"

Pattison describes six ways in which practitioners and others in the phenomenal world of the dying person can assist in creating an appropriate death:

1. Sharing the responsibility for the crisis of dying . . . so that he has help in dealing with the first impact of anxiety and bewilderment.
2. Clarifying and redefining the realities of the day-to-day existence which can be dealt with by the patient.
3. Making continued human contact available and rewarding.
4. Assisting in the separation from and grief over the realistic losses of family, body image, and self control, while retaining communication and meaningful relationships with those who will be lost.
5. Assuming necessary body and ego functions for the person without incurring shame or depreciation, maintaining respect for the person, and helping him maintain his self respect.
6. Encouraging the person to work out an acceptance of his life situation with dignity and integrity so that gradual regression may occur without conflict or guilt.

This paper began with a discussion of the process of learning of dying; the latter half dealt with tasks facing the dying. It is customary to close an article by stating that we do not presently have enough information and that we need additional research. I agree with that thought. Nonetheless, I think we do have enough information to put certain changes into effect, since the knowledge we have is superior to no knowledge at all. What we need is the ability to communicate our information in a sufficiently persuasive fashion to the decision-makers, i.e., every practitioner who works with the terminally ill. We need to communicate what we know about the ways in which people learn of their impending death and how they respond to this information; we need to communicate the significance of the tasks that face the dying and how to help them cope with the tasks. We need to persuade other practitioners that the dying person is as much a human being as he ever was and that he is entitled to the same consideration that was his due before the terminal diagnosis. And we need to become sufficiently comfortable with the inevitability of our own death so that we can help others learn to accept theirs.

REFERENCES

Diggory, James C. and Rothman, Doreen Z., "Values destroyed by death". *Journal of Abnormal and Social Psychology,* **63,** 205-210, 1961.

Glaser, Barney G. and Strauss, Anselm L., *Awareness of Dying,* Aldine, Chicago, 1965.

Glaser, Barney G. and Strauss, Anselm L., *Time for Dying,* Aldine, Chicago, 1968.

Pattison, E. Mansell, "Help in the dying process". *Voices: The Art and Science of Psychotherapy,* **5,** 6-14, 1969.

CHAPTER
3

The Dying Patient and the Double-Bind Hypothesis

Richard C. Erickson
and
Bobbie J. Hyerstay

Stories come to us from other times and places depicting death as a dramatic moment. Loved ones are gathered at the bedside and the poignant business of settling one's affairs and saying goodbyes is carried out with awesome dignity. A kind of winsome honesty is evident in Kübler-Ross's account of the death of a farmer [1] or the Asian custom of relatives gathering at the bedside of the dying patient two or more days before death is expected, "openly indicating to the patient that they are there to keep him company during his passage out of life" [2]. Granting a measure of romanticizing and a glossing over of unpleasant aspects in these reports, this manner of dying seems infinitely preferable to the impersonal, technological fate we can expect to face.

It is an unpleasant, but probably inevitable, fact of modern times that a majority can expect to die in institutional settings rather than in their own homes and that increasing numbers can expect to face death at the end of a prolonged decline [2]. It is also inevitable, although not aesthetically pleasing, to expect one's final illness to be invaded by cold hardware—the needles, tubes, wires, and consoles of life-saving, life-supporting, and pain-relieving apparatus. The setting for death could be warmer and more familiar, but in the balance, most would allow that it's a fair trade to increase their chance for survival and physical comfort.

Prevalent in many institutions caring for terminal patients, however, seems to be a consensus bordering on an informal policy that it is desirable and proper to conceal from the patient knowledge of his impending death. Information flows around the patient from doctor to staff to relatives as is deemed necessary, but elaborated precautions are often taken to protect the patient from the fact.

18

It is the intent of this paper to suggest that most attempts to conceal are not only misguided and futile, but also that they set in motion a brutal set of social interactions that are psychologically destructive to the patient.

It is probably the case that most patients know their condition whether they are told or not. Avorn [3] cites a study showing that 80% of terminal cancer patients know their diagnosis. Kübler-Ross [1] notes that the outstanding fact of her work with over 200 dying patients was that they all had an awareness of the seriousness of their condition whether they were told or not. Reeves [4] concluded on the basis of his experience that the terminal patient is rare who does not know "regardless of the protective fictions spun by staff and family." Feifel [5] reports that 82% of sample of patients wanted to know about their condition. Kelly and Friesen [6] questioned three groups of people. Eighty-nine per cent of a group of 100 cancer patients who had been told their diagnosis reported they would have preferred to be told. Eighty-two per cent of a group of 100 non-cancer patients reported they would want to know the truth if they had cancer. 98.5% of a group of 740 patients who were undergoing diagnostic tests at a cancer detection center indicated they wanted to be told the truth if they had cancer. Feifel [5] compared studies concerning whether or not to tell patients about their diagnosis. Depending upon the specific study, 69-90% of the physicians studied favored not telling. In an opposing vein, 77-89% of patients wanted to know.

Thus, it seems, an abundance of time and effort goes into producing an elaborate deception for an audience that 1) doesn't want to be deceived and 2) already suspects the grim denouement of the drama.

But setting aside for the moment whether the patient knows or wants to know, what in fact takes place when deception is undertaken? Briefly, an attempt is made to invest a terminal patient with a "fictional future biography" and control his assessment of cues and events that might lead him to suspect the truth [2, 7]. Staff, family, and even other patients may be directly or indirectly informed and enlisted so the proper behaviors are elicited. The deception presumes to encompass verbal and nonverbal levels.

Controlling verbal behavior would appear to be relatively easy, but, in point of fact, an elaborate system of evasions, double talk and falsehoods is necessary. Glaser and Strauss [2], among others, describe the intricate footwork attempted by staff: misleading explanations for medical decisions, hints and fabrications to suggest favorable progress, discounting symptoms, encouraging the patient to make optimistic interpretations, undue attention to irrelevant statements or events, reducing the range of expression and conversational topics, and focusing talk on the present. The task of keeping a number of staff cued in seems monumental. Inconsistencies will destroy the fiction unless specific measures are taken to transmit information to staff on another shift or to new staff. The sheer complexity of maintaining a consistent verbal facade on the part of the staff, let alone family and other patients, guarantees the eventual collapse of the enterprise if the patient lingers.

The futility of attempting deception is evident when one recognizes that every person also understands and responds to a concurrent set of nonverbal cues. In interpreting a message, a person also attends to the other's gestures, voice pitch and inflection, facial expressions, nonresponses, etc. The grammar of body language has been closely studied by Birdwhistell [8] among others. Body language may serve as an indicator of attitudes, status of relationships, degrees of anxiety being experienced, and may accentuate or contradict a verbal statement. For example, Dittman [9] found patterns of body movements indicative of a person's mood. As fleeting as nonverbal signals may be, they likely play a key role in making deception nearly impossible and conveying powerful expectancies affecting performance.

People receive and respond to nonverbal cues even though they may not be able to label or "put their finger on" what they are responding to. It is reasonable to say that people place at least as much, if not more, reliance on subtle, nonverbal cues as verbal cues. In fact, Mehrabrian [10] contends that 93% of the total communicative message is nonverbal.

Several investigators have observed and reported on an abundance of revealing nonverbal cues in the institutional setting [2, 7, 11-13]. The dying patient may be moved to a separate room, a room with a comatose patient, or a room at the end of the hall. There is a tendency to withdraw and have fewer direct communications with him. Staff and visitors behave in tight, constricted ways. Interactions are marked by shallow, brittle cheerfulness. Topics like death and the future are evaded. Visits may become shorter, more perfunctory, or may stop altogether. Extra doctors may appear and tests and procedures are carried out with little explanation given as to their specific purpose. There are tell-tale pauses, eyes that don't meet or drop, unexplained solicitude or privileges. Staff may tend to avoid the room or may look in and leave without coming in. Nurses take longer to respond to call lights from terminal patients. A quite marked pattern known as the "death watch" may be carried out by the nurse if she suspects the end is near. Strauss and Glaser have observed that staff and family organize themselves firmly around an assumed "dying trajectory" and they experience problems if the patient does not follow this pattern.

The sequence of nonverbal cues tells its own story. Unless we are willing to assume that the patient has forgotten what lifelong experience has taught him, we must conclude that he is more or less explicitly aware of this deception, or consuming a considerable amount of psychological energy to ignore it. A pathetic note is struck when the patient, aware of the deception, engages in mutual pretense with those attending him [7].

In short, we submit that it is untenable to assume that the truth can be withheld from a patient, i.e., that an elaborate fiction can be carried out for any length of time by a large company of people, none of whom has had a lesson in acting. Whether the patient will suspend his disbelief in response to a good act is questionable. If he does, it will cost him psychological energy to do so. Reality has a habit of continually insinuating itself.

Doctors and other medical staff are invested in trying to alleviate suffering, but often little emphasis is placed in their years of training on how to deal with the enormous crisis an awareness of impending death precipitates nor are they adequately prepared to operate in a context of accountability regarding the psycho-social aspects of death [2, 7]. Their intent is to provide an orderly, tranquil and hopeful setting for the dying patient and for other patients in the setting, and they must attempt this in the face of the most disturbing and disrupting event of all. Society expects them to deal with a reality it takes great pains to ignore. Granting their good intentions, it is tempting to conclude that they are making the best of an extremely difficult situation. Perhaps, in the final analysis, they cannot withhold the truth, but at least they have alleviated suffering in the attempt.

Unfortunately, a case can be made that attempts by the staff and family to protect the patient from his diagnosis and prognosis may, in fact, set in motion a set of social interactions that are psychologically destructive to the patient. To explain this, we will need to introduce the reader to the "double bind hypothesis" and its psychiatric consequences.

Briefly defined, the double bind is a situation "1) in which a person is faced with contradictory messages, 2) which is not readily visible as such because of concealment or denial or because messages are on different levels and 3) in which he can neither escape or notice and effectively comment on the contradictions" [14]. The inability to escape is the result of dependence on those giving the contradictory messages, a dependency inherent in childhood or illness.

A simple illustration of a double bind would be a mother saying "Come here, dear" to her child in a slightly hostile tone accompanied by slight bodily withdrawal. Nonverbal and verbal cues don't match, but attempts by the child to clarify meaning by calling attention to the incongruity are met with guilty denial or protests of benevolent concern on the part of the mother. Her attempts to cover up the first incongruity comprise another pair of incongruent messages and so on in a progressive and cumulative manner.

Double bind messages are common enough that most of us recognize them and deal with them using confrontation or humor. We seldom find ourselves sufficiently dependent or subjected to double binds as a recurrent theme. We probably experience them as a transient disruption in the flow of a relationship.

Bateson, Jackson, Haley and Weakland [15] suggest that, when a normal person is caught in a double bind situation, he will respond in a defensive manner similar to that of the schizophrenic. Given the double bind as a recurrent theme in a person's experience so that the double bind structure comes to be a habitual expectation, more serious effects may follow. The person may experience increasing difficulty in discriminating communication modes in the messages he receives from others, the messages he emits, or even within his own internal experience. The victim of the recurrent double bind may find himself unable to judge what others mean and resort to continually searching for hidden meanings detrimental to his welfare (paranoid), treating all messages as unimportant or to be laughed at (hebephrenic), or cutting off more and more interaction with the outside world (catatonic). Without help, the person cannot discover what people mean and is subject to a vicious cycle of distortions.

The classic double bind involves the ambivalent mother who emits hostile, withdrawing behavior when the child approaches and simulated loving or approaching behavior as a way of denying that she is withdrawing when the child responds accurately to her behavior. The mother needs to control her anxiety by controlling her distance from the child. "To put this another way, if the mother begins to feel affectionate and close to her child, she begins to feel endangered and must withdraw from him; but she cannot accept this hostile act and to deny it must simulate affection and closeness with her child" [15]. To discriminate, the child must see that the mother doesn't want him and is deceiving him by her loving behavior. All the while, the mother is "benevolently" defining for the child what is going on. The child is punished for correct and incorrect discriminations. And support from others is lacking or cut off.

Little wonder that the victim of a double bind situation experiences helplessness, fear, and rage and may respond with misinterpretations and distortions of reality, constricted and inappropriate emotional responsiveness, loss of empathy with others, and withdrawing or bizarre behavior (the diagnostic description for schizophrenia).

How all this applies to the terminal patient is perhaps becoming evident to the reader. A rereading of the preceding paragraphs substituting staff and/or family for mother and the terminal patient for child is disturbing in its appositeness. We hasten to underline the fact that this material is being presented as a hypothesis, not a demonstrated finding. Reports of interactions between staff and patient and family and patient are too sketchy and anecdotal to offer convincing support at this time. On the other hand, on the basis of published observations and the logic inherent in the situation, it is hard to see how any other interaction can prevail if the patient is not informed of his condition. The reader is invited to test his own experience.

The patient enters the hospital quite literally full of hopes and fears. The very act of entering expresses his willingness to place his life and well being in the hands of an institution and its personnel and his declaration that he sees this place and these people as noble, trustworthy, benevolent and full of life-saving powers. In submitting to treatment he is ascribing almost superhuman powers and rectitude to doctors and staff. At the same time, the act of entering constitutes an admission that he is facing a serious threat which he cannot handle by himself. He is at least apprehensive about how serious the threat is and may entertain the possibility that his life is in danger. Hospitals are not for run-of-the-mill diseases. In short, the patient is more dependent, less self-sufficient, more vulnerable and more apt to ascribe magical powers to powerful others than at any other time in his life save childhood. The mode of his interaction is childlike: "I'll do what you say. You must take care of me."

Medical staff are defined by themselves and society as those who are able to take care of sick people. Their task is to save lives, to prevent pain and anguish, to make people comfortable. They are expected to know how to handle things. Never mind their training or temperament. They always do what's best for the patient. "I will take care of you if you do what I say." So death signals a failure and manifest anguish arouses anxiety.

The doctor, most pressed for time, most responsible for the life or death of the patient, is alone granted the authority to withhold or permit revelation of the fact that the patient is about to die. Family and staff can be expected to defer to his spoken or implied wishes. They are unlikely to reveal the truth except with his expressed permission.

The scene is set. Doctor, staff, and family know. The patient does not. All are defining their role vis-a-vis patient in terms of benevolent concern. All approach the patient with anxiety and a host of ambivalent feelings. The patient is extraordinarily dependent and vulnerable, and the messages he receives are of the gravest significance.

The patient begins to pick up nonverbal cues that all is not well. But people keep talking reassuringly. He may be receiving alarming signals from his own body, but these are discounted. Something's wrong, but the evidence for it is so elusive. He can't quite put his finger on the discrepancies. Are visits really shorter, or does it merely seem that way? Is the atmosphere more ominous? Really? Why did the doctor pause that way? Why won't the nurse look me in the eyes? Surely they would say if something was wrong, or would they? The inconsistencies and incongruities pile up and the patient's apprehensions and suspicions increase.

Under the pressure of anxiety, the patient begins to formulate information—seeking questions, probably tactful and approximate. How will he gather evidence for the question, "Are things more serious than I've been told? Am I going to die?" He asks his tentative question of the nurse, or the nursing aide, seemingly innocent but loaded with importance. And the nurse refers him to the doctor, and/or comments with ritual, professional cheerfulness, "Don't you worry about a thing, you're doing just fine." If he tries to pursue it, he may notice subtle signs that the nurse is becoming anxious, and she may excuse herself prematurely and tend to avoid the room. If he comments on that, she will deny it and may appear confused or hurt. Yet, if he tries to go along with her verbal reassurance in any serious way, he again notices her discomfort or desire to withdraw from any but the most ritual interactions. Or the family. It's harder to raise the issue with them. It could cause them pain. But how forced and brittle with cheerfulness the visits are getting. If the patient hints of his apprehension, others, with a glance at one another, rush in with reassurance: "You'll be up in no time." But if he tries to approach them as if they had a future together, he notices that he arouses discomfort and precipitates withdrawal. If he tries to comment on that, he gets the message "You are to treat me like I want to be approached."

Reality continues to insinuate itself through repeated exposure. The patient's suspicions grow and apprehension gnaws at him. Yet no one will settle the issue. The patient begins to doubt himself, feeling he must be missing something. Others act as if the situation were quite logical and consistent. Every comment he makes on the situation seems in some way inappropriate. Something must be wrong with the way he's looking at things.

Should he ask the doctor? He has the authority to say. But consider the doctor's problem. He is most pressed for time. Who can and will deal with the patient's response to the revelation? He has his own anxieties about death. He was supposed to save this man's life—he has failed. On top of his own professional concerns and personal anxieties, he is expected by the family, staff, and perhaps the patient himself to manage so that the situation remains calm, orderly, and hopeful. More than any other person, the doctor is under pressure to evade and postpone revealing the truth. But because of his position, the incongruity in his messages arouses the greatest anxiety. The patient is ill and uncertain. "If the doctor knew, wouldn't he tell me? If he won't tell me, he must be afraid of how I would take it. Perhaps he knows I am dying and has reason to feel I can't handle the truth. Maybe I couldn't."

In order to get out of the bind, the patient is asked to take on an unbelievable task. He must, on his own, accept the fact he is dying and take the risk of expressing the metacommunicative message: "It is obvious to me you are uncomfortable and evasive around me because I am dying and you are having difficulty dealing with me as a dying person." Such a courageous act may be rewarded with the revelation of the truth and relief on everyone's part. But there is also a great risk that it will set in motion more spirited denial and concealment. The patient faces here the greatest threat that he will experience punishment in the form of anger, withdrawn love, avoidance, and abandonment. How will the doctor, staff and family deal with him when he violates the communication pattern so essential to their security? In fact, he is asking a great deal. Others must admit their own vulnerability and misguided efforts and rely on the dying patient to show strength and concern for them. They must be able to let the patient comfort them in their anxiety and grief.

In summary, then, while the patient may give out his own incongruent messages, this is of secondary importance since the family and staff are not so dependent and can escape the situation and find allies. The patient is deeply dependent on staff and family who may systematically convey the following incongruities: 1) on the verbal level and all controllable nonverbal levels, others attempt to propagate the fiction "You will live." The patient is enjoined (cf, the command aspect of the message [16]) to act confidently and hopefully, to make plans for the future, and to behave as if the present situation were a passing unpleasantry. 2) A pattern of nonverbal cues declares "You will die." The patient is enjoined to come to terms with this reality and to help others—staff and family—to be reconciled to the loss. An undercurrent is the emotional ambivalence on the part of the staff and family similar to that discussed above: they can neither approach or avoid comfortably.

A patient's attempt to respond to the verbal message, i.e., to decrease inter-personal distance by acting on the hypothesis that he will live, not only makes the nonverbal cues more evident, but compounds them as the other person's anxiety increases and he attempts to maintain and embellish the fiction. An attempt to respond to the nonverbal cues is met with denial and protests of benevolent concern. The terminal patient is called upon to distort his perception of reality in order to protect the feelings of the other person and incongruity is piled on incongruity in a progressive and cumulative manner.

When the patient lingers, the theme is recurrent and is played out with ever-increasing elaborateness. The institution may programatically deprive the patient of honest informants among staff, family or other patients [2], and he literally cannot leave the field.

At this point, we can anticipate the results observers will report. The patient approaches the time of death with an increasing sense that he has no one he can trust. He feels dishonored and abandoned, anxious and worried [3, 4]. "At a time when closeness is one of the only remaining sources of joy, it is undermined by an unacknowledged system of deceptions whose intricacy can reach Laingian dimensions" [3]. "A patient who is in a life and death crisis may also be caught in an antitherapeutic atmosphere, in which salient facts and perceptions are avoided and distorted. Consequently, he may slant his own communications and thoughts. Then, because people surrounding him mouth platitudes and truisms, the double-edged effect may be for everyone involved to repudiate each other, while remaining physically present and officially concerned. For example, if a dying person finds himself treated like a hopeless case or like a child who cannot understand, he may become hopeless about himself, plead that he does not understand, and be convinced that he is worthless as well" [17]. Strauss and Glaser [7] have commented that withdrawal and apathy may follow the unprogrammed revelation that death is imminent and the trusted family members have been part of the deception. Glaser and Strauss [2] and Reeves [4] have noted that, in the end, the patient may need to be stupefied by drugs to manage his behavior or to keep the truth from coming out.

A penultimate experience of abandonment and confusion: a terrible finale.

And largely because some scarcely tenable assumptions are made. 1) That a large number of people can effectively carry out an elaborate deception for an extended period of time in the face of a suspecting audience. 2) That revelation of the truth is the only painful or most painful course of action others can carry out. Glaser and Strauss [2] comment on how these assumptions are perpetuated by medical folklore.

An attempt to maintain tranquility in the face of death is similar to the attempt by an estranged couple to smooth over the rift. It only exacerbates the problem. It is certainly true that the truth will precipitate an emotional crisis, but, as any psychotherapist will testify, the pain of expressing pent-up feelings is far preferable to bottling them up in an insidious context of deception and distortion. In the balance, it must be acknowledged that the crisis is disturbing and time-consuming. Family and staff must be prepared to invest time and emotional energy.

But patients do work through the crisis [1] and the possibility opens up for loved ones to share honest last few days together [3], and patients can even give support to one another and to the staff [7].

We are not suggesting that the terminal patient is to be told the truth with all due haste and bluntness. There are weighty issues to take into account which have been sensitively discussed at length elsewhere [18]. We are suggesting that deception is usually a futile and destructive strategy. The task facing the staff is how to present to the patient tactfully and with sensitivity that he is probably going to die at the juncture where staff usually begins to implement their deceptions. All the elaborate effort and good will which go into withholding the truth should rather go into revealing the truth. The skill required is similar to that of the psychotherapist who neither bluntly confronts his patient with the truth from the first moment he, the therapist, apprehends it, but neither does he establish or participate in the patient's self deceptions. Rather the therapist bends his efforts to lead the patient to the discovery of the truth about himself.

How might our hospitals be modified and their staff be encouraged to respond more personally, more individually, more humanly to the dying person and his family? How might they be designed to help alleviate the double-binding "no exit" situation in which the dying patient may find himself?

Changes might be made within the design of the physical structure itself. Places which provide opportunities for patients and/or their families to engage in either private conversations or more intimate caring relationships would be a significant beginning. How can a person share his very inner most, intimate thoughts and feelings of impotence, anger, grief, and helplessness in a two- or four-bed ward? Difficult, at best! There is isolation in hospitals, but little privacy. Day rooms that invite conversation with others could also be a place where patients and their families could gain support and understanding from each other.

Allowances could be made for live-in situations which are now only accorded the rich. Arrangements could be made for spouses to stay with the patient through those particularly stressful periods when it would be comforting to have the hand of someone close to you to touch for reassurance. This could significantly help the patient deal with his fears of being rejected and abandoned.

Every patient who enters a hospital is expected to unlearn many of the roles which have become so familiar to him and go into making up his identity as a person. He is expected to assume the role of the patient. As institutions are unlikely to change greatly, counselors could assist in interpreting and clarifying with the patient and his family what is going on, what is expected of him, by talking to and with him rather than around and about him. Nothing is more devastating to one's individuality and identity than to be referred to as the "colostomy in Rm. 8."

Being able to bring familiar items from home may also help to take some of the strangeness and unfamiliarity out of the hospital situation. Merely wearing one's own pajamas or laying one's head down on a familiar pillowcase can make a difference when everything else about one is foreign and threatening. Some familiar items are important because they give one a known base from which to begin to tentatively explore new awarenesses and realities.

Rules which prohibit children from visiting their parents may be appropriate to the physical needs of the patient; but are often devastating to the psychological relationship and needs of both child and parent.

It is important that the patient be involved in the planning and decision making processes of his treatment. Having the ability to make input and decisions is an essential part of gaining and maintaining one's individual identity. Explaining what medical procedures, tests, medication and medical terms mean to the patient can begin to reduce some of the ambiguity of the situation. Involving the patient as an active agent in his own treatment can enable him to trust those around him. He can get a better grasp on the reality of his situation rather than having to fabricate his own reality or psychologically withdraw. Forming trusting relationships is one of the most effective ways to encourage open communication.

In addition to the attending physician, an interdisciplinary team including a counselor or psychologist, a social worker, a minister, a recreational therapist and a nurse could be specifically designated to respond to the various needs of the dying patient and his family. As non-medical personnel, they are not conflicted over their "failure" to save the patient's life. The team could focus on the "whole person." The psychologist could meet with dying patients as individuals and in groups and with their families to help them work through their emotions about the impending death. The social worker could help the patient and his family work out the concrete financial and social problems posed by this drastic change of circumstance. He could also serve as a liaison and an advocate for the patient with other staff and services in the hospital. The social worker would be a key component in helping the patient to understand and adjust to the complex hospital community.

A recreational therapist may seem a strange component on such a team, but pleasure needs of the dying person and his family are sadly neglected. Attendance to individually declared needs may help the patient gain some perspective on his situation and enable him to cope with the long hours in the hospital. A minister would be helpful to responding to the spiritual needs of the individual. A nurse could interpret the "unintelligible" medical terms, tests and procedures to the dying patient as well as providing a liaison with the attending physician. Even patients who are quite ill can benefit from group interaction with the assurance that a nurse is close by if they need her.

Such a team could provide the supportive *core* to which a patient and his family could turn as they try to clarify, understand, and integrate the complexities of the entire situation. It would be the goal of the team to help the patient and his family to live as fully and meaningfully as possible while at the same time assisting them in coping with the many tasks of an individual's dying.

Many have spoken of the need for specialized training for medical personnel in how to respond to the psychosocial needs of the dying patient. The point will not be belabored here. But few have addressed the equally important needs of medical staff, from the physician to the nursing aide. They need an outlet for the feelings of frustration, anger, helplessness and grief that they may experience in caring for the dying person. Counseling services should be provided for staff members who are constantly charged with the task of saving lives, an ultimately impossible task. Medical staff members should have an opportunity to share their thoughts and feelings in a supportive atmosphere, so they can in turn be responsive and supportive to the patient and his family.

Essentially, we are speaking of designing an institution and forming a staff that are person-centered. With a more humanistically-oriented institution and staff, it is hoped that the patient might look forward to receiving support and acceptance in his sharings and an "exit" from a double-binding situation. The patient is given an ample opportunity to test with a *core* of others (an interdisciplinary team) what he perceives as reality in an open, honest, supportive way, making it unnecessary for him to resort to a defensive schizophrenic-like reaction to cope with the situation.

REFERENCES

1. Kübler-Ross, Elisabeth, *On Death and Dying*, New York: Macmillan, 1969.
2. Glaser, B. G. and Strauss, A. L., *Awareness of Dying*, Chicago: Aldine, 1965, 3-46.
3. Avorn, Jerry, "Beyond Dying." *Harper's*, March 1973, 246(1474): 56-64.
4. Reeves, R., "To tell or Not to Tell the Patient," in A. H. Kutscher, (ed.), *Death and Bereavement*, Springfield, Ill.: Chas. C. Thomas, 1964.
5. Feifel, Herman, "Death," in N. L. Faberow, (ed.), *Taboo Topics*, New York: Atherton, 1963, 8-21.
6. Kelly, W. D. and Friesen, J., "Do Cancer Patients Want to be Told?" *Surgery*, 1950, 27, 822-826.

7. Strauss, A. L. and Glaser, B. G., "Patterns of Dying" in O. Brim, et al, (eds.), *The Dying Patient,* New York: Russell Sage Foundation, 1970, 129-155.
8. Birdwhistell, R. L., *Kinesics and Context*, Philadelphia: University of Pennsylvania Press, 1970.
9. Dittman, A. T., "The Relationship Between Body Movement and Moods in Interviews," *Journal of Consultive Psychiatry*, 1962, 26(5): 480.
10. Mehrabrian, A., "Communication Without Words," *Psychology Today*, September 1968, 2(4): 52.
11. Sudnow, D., "Dying in a Public Hospital," in O. Brim, et al., (eds.), *The Dying Patient*, New York: Russell Sage Foundation, 1970, 191-208.
12. LeShan, L., cited in Bowers, M., Jackson, E. N., Knight, J. A., and LeShan, L., *Counseling the Dying*, New York: Thomas Nelson, 1964, 6-7.
13. Kalish, R. A., "Social Distance and the Dying," *Community Mental Health Journal*, 1966, 2: 152-155.
14. Weakland, J. H., "The Double Bind Hypothesis of Schizophrenia and Three Party Interaction," in D. D. Jackson, (ed.), *The Etiology of Schizophrenia*, New York: Basic Books, 1960, 373-388.
15. Bateson, G., Jackson, D. D., Haley, J., and Weakland, J., "Toward a Theory of Schizophrenia," in G. D. Shean, (ed.), *Studies in Abnormal Behavior*, Chicago: Rand McNally, 1971, 252-271.
16. Haley, J., *Strategies of Psychotherapy*, New York: Grune and Stratton, 1963.
17. Weisman, A. D., *On Death and Denying*, New York: Behavioral Publications, Inc., 1972.
18. Pemberton, L. B., "Diagnosis: Ca—Should We Tell the Truth," *Bulletin of the American College of Surgeons*, 1971, 56, 7-13.

CHAPTER
4

Clinical Research and
the Stages of Dying[1]

Richard Schulz and David Aderman

Attitudes toward death tend to vary as a function of the patient's temporal location in the dying process. Some authors feel that predictable attitudes emerge in a "stages of death" model while others feel the process is less rigid and even stageless.

Probably the strongest and most popular advocate of a "stage theory" of dying has been Elisabeth Kübler-Ross [1]. In *On Death and Dying*, Kübler-Ross outlined a five-stage process of dying based on her observations of 200 patients, 197 of whom she attributes as having completed the process prior to death.

According to Kübler-Ross, the patient's initial response to learning that he is terminal is shock and numbness. This state is gradually replaced by the first distinct stage in the dying process—*denial*. The patient's reaction at this stage is, "No, not me; it cannot be true." Thus, a patient who is convinced that his x-rays or his lab reports were mixed up with someone else's would be classified in the denial stage. Kübler-Ross argued that this stage is adaptive in that it acts as a "buffer after the unexpected shocking news, allows the patient to collect himself and, with time, mobilize other, less radical defenses [1, p. 39]."

Denial is said to be followed by *anger*. Patients at this stage are angry because their plans and activities have been interrupted, and they envy those who can still enjoy life. Frequently, the patient asks, "Why me? Why couldn't it have been somebody else?" From the staff and the family's point of view, this stage is more troublesome than the previous stage since the patient's anger is directed almost randomly at anyone in his environment. Kübler-Ross stressed that staff and family must avoid responding personally to anger directed at them.

Bargaining, the third stage in the model, is relatively short. Having been angry

[1] Preparation of this report was facilitated by Grant GS-35175 from the National Science Foundation.

at people and God in the previous stage, the patient now believes that he "can succeed in entering some sort of agreement which may postpone the inevitable happening [1, p. 83]." Usually the patient offers good behavior (e.g., fervent prayer) in exchange for a postponement of death, but once a specific deadline is reached the patient begins bargaining all over again, asking for more time. Kübler-Ross provided an example of a patient at the bargaining stage who asked for enough time to attend her eldest son's wedding. She left the hospital the day of the wedding, returned the next day, and began bargaining again, this time for enough time to attend her second son's wedding.

An anticipated or actual physical loss usually brings on the fourth postulated stage—*depression*. Depression may be the result of increased symptoms or the realization that one is becoming weaker and thinner. Surgical procedures such as the removal of a breast or part of the face often result in deep depression. According to Kübler-Ross, a patient should be encouraged to work through this anguish and, in so doing, reach the final stage in the dying process.

The final stage is *acceptance*. "If a patient has had enough time ... and has been given some help in working through the previously described stages, he will reach a state during which he is neither depressed nor angry about his 'fate' [1, pp. 112-113]."

Kübler-Ross completed her analysis with the observation that a little hope runs through all five stages, and that patients are aware of the seriousness of their illness whether or not so informed. All patients, according to Kübler-Ross, have the opportunity to work through the stages and achieve a good death. Although some patients reach the acceptance stage without the aid of others, most need assistance. The Kübler-Ross message, then, is that medical personnel and family members should be sensitive to whatever stage a dying patient is in and, if necessary, work with the patient to reach the acceptance stage.

Unfortunately, the usefulness of Kübler-Ross's work is limited by its ambiguity, in large part the product of the highly subjective manner in which observations were obtained and interpreted. Kübler-Ross failed to explicitly specify assessment procedures for determining through which stages of dying a patient has passed. Judging from the interview protocols Kübler-Ross has presented as evidence in support of her stage model, it appears that she depended more on intuition to define a particular stage than any systematic pattern of responses from the patient. Because misperceiving a stage could result in negative consequences for the patient (e.g., earlier death), it is crucial that the stages be clearly and easily identified. It is also important to know whether dying patients necessarily go through each stage in the particular sequence described by Kübler-Ross or whether they may jump from one stage to another, skipping one or more in between. Clearly, the stages have little predictive value if one cannot easily specify the stage an individual is in and the stage that is to follow.

While Kübler-Ross based her conclusions on information obtained through highly subjective personal interaction with over 200 dying patients, other researchers [2, 3, 4, 5, 6] have attempted to plot the emotional trajectory of the dying patient with more objective methods. Hinton [2], for example, assessed mood, physical distress, level of consciousness, and awareness of dying in approximately 70 dying patients who were interviewed at weekly intervals. Data collected during the last eight weeks each patient lived were analyzed.

A large portion of the sample (nearly 90%) experienced physical distress, requiring the administration of "a popular and effective mixture of morphine and cocaine [2, p. 14]." Although Hinton acknowledged that the drug administered to the patient may have produced side-effects of altered mood and decreased level of consciousness, he made no attempt to document the extent of this influence. Among all patients, impairment of consciousness increased steadily from 20% at week eight to 55% shortly before death. Among those patients who remained conscious, depression was found in half the patients throughout the eight weeks, increasing in the last two weeks of life. Anxiety was less prevalent but showed a similar increase the last two weeks of life.

Expectations of death were generally low among conscious patients. Only 20% of these patients were certain that they were going to die a week before death while another 20% thought that death was probable within this time period. The remaining patients had not mentioned death at all or had only spoken of the possibility of dying.

That Hinton and Kübler-Ross both used nondirected interviews to collect their data should make their results all the more comparable. Both investigators observed increased depression shortly before death, but only Hinton acknowledged the possibility that drugs may have influenced this finding. Undoubtedly Kübler-Ross's patients were conscious when interviewed, but at the same time, some of them at least, may have been taking drugs which altered mood. The depression she associated with the increased severity of physical symptoms, for instance, may simply have been the result of increased doses of drugs given to alleviate the new or more severe symptoms.

Hinton assessed general anxiety as a separate dimension in his patients, but Kübler-Ross viewed it as something that is present in many patients throughout several of the early stages although not in the final acceptance stage. Since Hinton found increased anxiety shortly before death, the data from the two studies do not agree here.

Another disparity is found in the data on the patient's awareness of his condition. Kübler-Ross reported that all of her patients knew they were terminal, while Hinton claimed that only 40% of his patients felt that their death was probable. Perhaps the other 60% of Hinton's patients also knew of their impending death but were merely denying it. If this is true, however, then another disparity comes to light. Patients who, according to Kübler-Ross should be at or near the acceptance stage, are still denying according to Hinton.

Regardless of interpretation, it is difficult to reconcile the two sets of observations. One might take the position that such disparities are to be expected given different populations of patients, but such an argument negates the value of this line of research.

Achte [3] compared a group of terminal cancer patients with a group of controls who also had cancer but were not terminal. The higher frequency of depression in the terminal group was the biggest difference between the two groups, although anxiety and tension were also more frequent among terminal patients. These findings are generally consistent with those reported by Hinton and Kübler-Ross.

Aggressiveness was frequently observed in the subgroup where the illness terminated quickly. These aggressive patients would seem to resemble most closely the Kübler-Ross patients in the denial and anger stages. Apparently, however, their deaths occurred before they had passed through the remaining Kübler-Ross stages.

Consistent with Hinton's findings, Achte reported that of those patients who died, 50% were unaware of the nature of their illness. Again, lack of awareness can be interpreted as repression or denial.

Lieberman [4] studied 25 men and women volunteers from a home for the aged. Subjects were given a series of tests and questionnaires at three-to-four-week intervals over a two-and-one-half year period. Since eight of his subjects died from eight months to two years after the study was begun, he was able to go back and determine whether or not the responses of subjects who died (Death Imminent Group—DIG) differed from those who did not die (Death Delayed Group—DDG).

The assessment devices which Lieberman used included the Bender-Gestalt test, the Draw-a-Person test, a time reproduction task, and a projective test in which the subject was asked to respond to 12 line drawings. With these tools Lieberman hoped to measure ego and cognitive functioning and affective states over time. Only his significant findings will be discussed here.

At the onset of the experimental period the two groups were found to differ significantly on only the area score of the Bender-Gestalt test. The DIG had an initially smaller Bender-Gestalt area score than the DDG. Presumably this is an indication that the DIG had less "available energy that is free for dealing with stimuli from the outer world [4, p. 182]." That is, they were unable to cope adequately with environmental demands. Results could not be accounted for by differences in physical illness.

The most significant finding of this study was the marked change in performance relative to initial scores of the DIG. These subjects showed a "decreased level of organization as measured by the adequacy of the Bender-Gestalt reproductions, a decreased energy as indicated by measurement of the size of the Bender-Gestalt figures, and a lessened ability to integrate stimuli as shown by a decrease in the complexity of the figure drawings [4, p.

189]." Only affective states, as measured by the projective technique described above, were not found to be systematically related to approaching death.

Lieberman attributed the decreased ability of individuals in the DIG to organize and integrate stimuli in their environment to a "general system decline" which is reflected in a variety of both physiological and psychological measures. Their ability to receive external stimuli impinging upon them did not decrease but their ability to interpret and deal with these stimuli was impaired, leaving them with the frightening impression that they were at the mercy of a chaotic world.

Lieberman used this same line of reasoning to explain the tendency for individuals approaching death to draw away from others and to isolate themselves. In his view, they do not withdraw because of "narcissistic preoccupation with themselves, but because they are preoccupied in an attempt to hold themselves together—to reduce the experience of chaos [3, p. 189]."

It is not unlikely that the behavior Lieberman calls withdrawal is interpreted as depression by other investigators. If this is the case, then it can be concluded that all four studies reviewed to this point agree on one thing—all terminal patients exhibit behavior indicating withdrawal or depression shortly before dying. Two related explanations for this kind of behavior have been suggested. Kübler-Ross claimed that depression results when the patient experiences an increase in the severity of his symptoms or loses some body part. Lieberman felt that depression may have its source in the physical decline of the patient which results in decreased ability to make sense of and deal with environmental stimuli. Both factors probably operate.

With the exception of the data on withdrawal, Lieberman's results differ from all the other data presented in that he found no affective differences between the DIG and the DDG; nor did he find any temporal changes in affective states of patients in the DIG. Two methodological features of Lieberman's study may have contributed to his rather unique findings. First, Lieberman used a projective technique to assess affective state rather than direct interview. The possibility of the interviewer becoming intimate with the patient and therefore learning more about feelings was undoubtedly greater in the studies employing direct interviews. Given the formality of the tests Lieberman administered and the fact that interviewers were replaced half way through the study, it is unlikely that the patient achieved intimacy with his interviewer. Secondly, Lieberman administered his tests at three-to-four-week intervals over a two-and-one-half year period, while the time intervals were much shorter in Hinton's and Küber-Ross's studies. (Hinton collected data at weekly intervals, and Kübler-Ross presumably visited her patients every day.) It is possible, then, that affective changes occurred in the Lieberman study, but remained undetected.

A very different approach to the study of the terminal phase of an individual's life has been taken by Weisman and Kastenbaum [5, 6]. Using a procedure called the psychological autopsy, these authors attempted to reconstruct the final phases of life for a patient. Their procedure involved an interdisciplinary conference in which information about a recently deceased patient was presented and discussed with the aim of studying the psychosocial context in which the death occurred.

After reviewing 80 cases over a five year period Weisman and Kastenbaum [5] concluded that patients entering the terminal period could be separated into two groups on the basis of their responses to impending death. One group seemed to be aware of and accept impending death. Most of these patients withdrew from daily activities, and remained inactive until the end. The other group was also aware of the prospect of imminent death but chose to vigorously engage in daily life activities and even to initiate new activities and interpersonal relationships. Death for these individuals came as an interruption in daily living. Fear of dying was observed rarely and then only in patients who were grossly impaired. Kastenbaum and Weisman [6] reported a similar pattern of response in another sample of 35 cases. In this latter sample, it was also found that the group that withdrew was older (89 vs. 81.5 years old) and had a shorter hospital stay (20 vs. 37.5 months) before death than the group that remained active. Since data on cognitive functioning are not reported it can be speculated that the two patterns of behavior are at least in part the result of different levels of cognitive ability. Like Lieberman's DIG patients the older group may have been less capable of coping with their environment and therefore withdrew from daily living while the younger group still had the capacity and motivation to engage in everyday activities.

Although these data were collected and interpreted post hoc and must therefore be viewed with some caution, the findings again cast doubt on the validity of a stage theory. Patients were not observed to go through stages but rather to adopt a pattern of behavior which persisted until death occurred.

SUMMARY

On the basis of her interviews with terminally ill patients, Kübler-Ross proposed a five-stage model of the dying process. Other investigators, relying less on clinical insight and more on objective measurement, have reported data which call into question the validity of Kübler-Ross's observations. Whereas these researchers have generally found, in agreement with Kübler-Ross, that most terminal patients experience depression shortly before death, they have failed to obtain any consistent evidence that other affect dimensions also characterize the dying patient.

As the disparity in current findings indicates, very little is really known about the process of dying. All that can be stated at present is that the dying patient's physical and cognitive functions deteriorate and that he is characteristically depressed and perhaps anxious about death. Obviously, much more research will be required to achieve a satisfactory understanding of this last phase of life.

REFERENCES

1. Kübler-Ross, E. *On death and dying*. New York: Macmillan Co., 1969.
2. Hinton, J. M. The physical and mental distress of dying. *Quarterly Journal of Medicine*, 1963, 32, 1-21.
3. Achte, K. A., and Vauhkonen, M. L. Cancer and the psyche. *Omega*, 1971, 2, 46-56.
4. Lieberman, M. A. Psychological correlates of impending death: Some preliminary observations. *Journal of Gerontology*, 1965, 20, 181-190.
5. Weisman, A. D., and Kastenbaum, R. The psychological autopsy; a study of the terminal phase of life. *Community Mental Health Journal*, 1968, Monograph No. 4.
6. Kastenbaum, R., and Weisman, A. D. The psychological autopsy as a research procedure in gerontology. In D. P. Kent, R. Kastenbaum, and S. Sherwood (Eds.), *Research planning and action for the elderly*. New York: Behavioral Publications, 1972.

CHAPTER
5

Slow Death: One
Survivor's Experience

Dorothy Paulay

Each of us is destined to be a survivor. Death awaits all of us, of course, but for practically everyone death will be experienced first as a survivor, as someone near or known to us dies. Our reactions to these deaths, along with the culture, race, mores, customs and ethics of our times, will help to shape our feelings toward our own death. While much has been written recently about the problem in our death-denying culture of coming to terms with the fact of death, for the most part discussion has been in terms of adjusting to the death of a loved one which has just occurred, or to one's own death which is imminent.

But there are many kinds of survivors, just as there are many kinds of deaths. Research has shown that practically everyone desires a quick, clean death with minimal suffering and no or very short illness. The individual prefers that for his loved ones too, although not so suddenly that there is no warning, no preparation time to adjust to unanticipated loss. Sometimes, however, there is no choice. The death is not quick and painless. Instead, there is the slow, inexorable debilitation of a chronic illness or traumatic injury through which both patient and family must suffer. The survivors of such a death go through a different qualitative experience of death and dying, especially if the process takes not days or weeks, but years. It is worsened by the process of being forced to watch the disintegration and loss of the image of the loved one as he slowly dies.

As members of the helping profession, we can expect to meet increasing numbers of persons directly affected by such experiences, as technology continues to enable the quantity, if not the quality, of life to be prolonged. As patients bring their experiences to our consultation rooms, we will be forced into increasing confrontation with our own feelings, attitudes, fears and anxieties about death and dying. We will have to depend on the experiences of others to help us to work through these feelings so that we can face the necessary explorations with minimal distress. The following is one therapist's account of her own personal, intimate experience with dying in confronting the lingering death of her husband. I have written it in order to describe one survivor's working through process and to offer whatever insights were gained which might be useful in helping other survivors of similar long-term illness and death of a loved one.

I suddenly became a member of our death-denying society, when I learned that my husband Jean was in a car accident. It was a head-on collision — both cars were completely demolished — both drivers were alone — Jean was unconscious under the wheel. The driver of the other car was found walking around. Both men were taken to a hospital. The other patient was discharged within three days with slight bruises. Jean remained in a coma for a week. Luck had chosen its victim in this encounter.

As a clinical social worker I had often listened and helped others cope with severe life stresses and with death. I know that a patient goes through a series of stages in his struggle with his fatal illness and that his family also goes through stages in accepting it. But while I had been able to help others, I found that I couldn't help myself. I couldn't accept the doctor's statement that Jean's brain was partially damaged and that he could never again be as I had known him. I denied the seriousness of Jean's illness, the degree to which he had been injured. It is through this experience that I really learned about my attitude toward life, death and dying.

I was filled with anger at what had happened, at luck which had singled us out for its cruelest of blows, which had robbed a man of all his abilities, and a family of its husband and father.

I directed my anger at the medical profession. I know doctors are human. They get sick and sometimes even die. At the hospital the doctor in charge of emergencies said that Jean was terminal. He didn't want me to see him. He felt the sight of the injury might be too much to take. I insisted on seeing him. Reluctantly the doctor directed me to a small room where he was lying on a table. He had plunged from the height of agility and health to the depths of total paralysis. Normally slender, his swollen body looked large, heavy; his face was covered with cuts. I stayed with him a few minutes and left.

That day and the rest of the week I remained around the hospital, waiting for him to regain consciousness. I wanted to be there when he came back to life to start him immediately on the road to recovery. I was filled with resolve. No matter how badly hurt Jean was, I would help him as I had helped others. But this was more blind wish than understanding. With only part of his brain functioning, my husband was severely disabled for five and one-half years until his death from pneumonia.

Even in the face of the doctor's hopeless attitudes, our thirteen-year-old son, Pete, and I retained the belief that he would recover. We were determined to help him do so and we were partially successful. For four years Pete and I devoted ourselves to caring for Jean. He relearned to walk and talk. At times he was rational, aware of his disability, sometimes grateful and appreciative of our attention, and sometimes angry, confused and depressed. He was aware of how much he had lost and showed great courage in facing the loss of everything that had been meaningful. For some it takes the form of hopelessness; for others it can be used to discover untapped inner strengths.

As if to support our own need to deny, we received numerous phone calls and letters expressing shock, sorrow and deep concern over Jean's condition. These wishes to be with us in spirit nourished and supported me. Letters reminded me that "Jean possesses the strength and will to get well." Another letter: "With his tremendous vitality and zest, if anyone has the spirit or will to accomplish the impossible, Jean will do it." From a rabbi: "I have seldom asked the God I serve to counter the laws of nature, but I would gladly forgive and praise Him for any miracle that might restore Jean to his charming, ebullient, capable, thoughtful self."

My efforts to cope with the situation were mostly denial — a "splitting off" of emotions. My personal life shrank. I limited my interest in the outside world to only those people or things that had a direct bearing on my immediate situation. I lived in the present only — concern about the future came later. I also became aware of my reaction to the way others acted toward me and toward Jean. I got a great lift from people's interest in Jean and their hope for him. When they seemed to give up, I was angry that he no longer merited their hope. I felt some people were uncomfortable in my presence, and their distress created discomfort in me. The more anxious they became, the more I felt their wish to avoid me. My ability to reach out or to receive expressions of human feelings decreased.

At the time of the accident, three doctors stated that Jean could not last the day. One doctor, trying to be objective, decided the unvarnished facts were best for me. He said, "He won't live. If he does he will be blind and totally paralyzed — a vegetable." As I look back now I realize I wanted to be told the truth in spite of my denial, my inability to face possible death. But I also desperately needed some spark of hope. Miracles sometimes happen. Truth can be cold, brutal, cruel. It should be tempered with gentleness and empathy.

Sometimes the denial in the family is its only defense to help it get through the crises, to give it time to integrate an unhappy truth. I didn't want to talk about Jean's impending death. I didn't want to admit he was dying. I couldn't. I preferred denial. Some of the doctors didn't understand and, therefore, didn't allow it.

As Jean slowly regained consciousness his doctor asked me what language he was speaking. I didn't know. I consulted his brother and learned that he was reciting the atonement prayer in Hebrew. Jean's background was that of an orthodox Jew. At age thirteen he had rebelled against religious rituals, which had no apparent meaning to him, and against the Hebrew language which he didn't understand. But he returned to partial life by traveling the tortured pathways of ingrained ancient customs with the Hebrew prayer of atonement.

When Jean was semi-conscious, I could at times reach him. This gave me hope that through our relationship I could help him get well, a hope I needed desperately. A sick person seldom gets well alone — he is helped by a give-and-take relationship. Unless there is some shred of hope, the survivor is hard put to be helpful. As Jean was regaining consciousness he suddenly would ask, "Why are you here?" And I would say, "Because I love you." One day he asked the question and I, feeling tired and discouraged, said, "Because I am here." To my surprise he corrected me with, "Say, because I love you." I thus became aware of how much he needed my love and support.

When he was moved from the hospital to a sanitarium, and tube feeding was discontinued, he reached Nirvana — "This is heaven, who found this place — excellent food." Then, thoughtfully, "Hope it doesn't cost too much." I admired his drive and determination to get well. My own hope was reinforced by his warmth, his humor, his optimism, his thoughtful self. "I will get well," he would say. "Some day we will see the world together." At other times he asked, "What makes you feel so sure that I will get well, and when I do, how will I feel?" He would say, "Tell me from the beginning what happened. Tell me all you know and that way I too will know." He would ask questions in an attempt to orient himself to the present, past and future. He would then say, "Be patient with me and my questions. I ask so I have someone to blame if it doesn't come out right." When I looked and felt low, he was kind. When I acted strong, he was hostile and angry.

As the months wore on, his personality became moody, alternating between elation and sadness. Sometimes he was frustrated, agitated, angry. I found notes he had written expressing his confusion and depression.

> "I love life and love it dearly, but today I am a lost man. Get better, for what? Why is life cruel? I am not cruel — why make life so? I am good — why isn't life equally so?"

He would say:

> "The only thing I know is what I don't know. I cannot fill the void. I feel so uncertain. Strange to lose one's memory. I am human — I am not getting better — I am getting worse. Tell me, who was the man I talked with? Strange that a mind can't make itself understood. I feel alone and lost. I am not concerned over not walking, but I am concerned about the confusion of my mind. People can see that I can't walk; they can't see my confused mind."

Jean felt himself an unworthy burden and was ashamed of his inability to function. Sometimes he viewed his illness as a punishment for real or imagined misdeeds. He was terrified at being abandoned now that he was sick. He felt alone and unlovable. He would say:

> "Life to me is very troublesome because I am a burden to you. I always have been independent. I don't want my life to be dependent on you. I must gain strength so I don't tire so quickly, so I can walk and use my right hand."

When the feeling in his hand returned he was overjoyed. "I feel like a new man — no longer a cripple."

Our son, Pete, was excellent with Jean. He helped him regain his physical strength and emotional worth. Jean was so proud of him as expressed by his notes: "Pete, I am fortunate to have you as my son." Another note; "Pete was like a breath of spring. The young man has an air of maturity that gives me a feeling of proudness. I can only give him my love and tell him he is wanted and loved by his mother and father."

Pete would try to help Jean by allowing him to do whatever he thought he could do himself: to recover feelings of self worth; to feel accepted and wanted. We were honest and direct. We pulled for him and with him. We tried to be tolerant and understanding of his inconsistent behavior, his frustrations, his helplessness.

We helped him recover from his aphasic period, a complicated condition affecting the ability to use or understand speech. In this aphasic period, he had an intense need to repeat a certain word over and over. Being a good speller, he spelled out words. He was aware of words coming out wrong, but with only part of his brain working he had no control over the words. There were reverses, opposites of what he meant. Sometimes he did not want to reveal how mixed up he was. He asked for sugar; given sugar, he had meant butter, so he sprinkled sugar over bread. Match for cigarette — napkin for blanket. He would say, "cold hot air," "dark sunshine outside," "election results are bad for the winner." "When you exhaust your sleep, you're well slept out." "I wouldn't wish this on my worst enemy that I like." We frequently laughed with him, when he realized what actually had come out instead of what he meant.

Jean's behavior reflected his inconsistent and often poor judgment. He set fires, tore magazines. At times he was noisy and belligerent. He had poor control over his anger and anxiety. He might start with a good idea but would end up applying it inappropriately. This behavior did not make him popular in sanitariums. They would request that he be removed, and I would have to start another search for a new sanitarium. Several times I found a new one where he would be the first patient and could remain until the sanitarium was filled. Then again I would be asked to move him.

In the fourth year of Jean's illness, Pete started a conversation with "When Daddy gets well . . ." I suddenly heard myself, "Daddy may never get well," and Pete said, "That's what I have been thinking." It was the first time that we could say aloud this fear of permanent disability — death — that we had denied, pushed aside for over four years.

It was the turning point in my life. I lost hope for my husband's recovery, then redirected it to rebuilding our family life. I redistributed my time and my energy and started to cope at last with the reality of Jean's illness. I continued to care for him, to arrange satisfactions to fill his limited life, but my hopes and goals were directed in rebuilding my own life and in separating myself from the impossible struggle to overcome his disabling illness by sheer will power. Having experienced Jean's struggle with life, I have learned that death is not always an "enemy" — sometimes it is a friend. It can be an end to a long life; it can sometimes be regarded as a privilege earned by intense suffering. I found comfort in Freud's attitude toward the person who had died: "admiration for someone who has accomplished a very difficult task." "Death," he said, "was a friendly idea."

I learned that fear of dying is not only human, a feeling I need not be ashamed of, but something I can learn to handle. Fear of death may be more a problem for the living than for the dying.

I have learned the hard way that my way of feeling is not the universal way. There is no one way of coping with dying. There is no "ought to feel" or "ought to be." Each person looks at life and death with a different set of values. There is gratifying richness in the variety of individual differences.

Late one night, Jean's doctor, who had proved most helpful to me, phoned. The sanitarium had called him to visit Jean. The doctor reported Jean had pneumonia with a 105° fever and that I should be prepared for the ending. Doctors on three previous occasions had prepared me for his death. I had not been ready to separate from him those times, and I didn't. This time I let him go — freed him. I cried the rest of the night.

Early next morning I was at the sanitarium. To my amazement I found Jean up walking around the room in an angry, complaining, demanding mood — fever normal. I remained with him that morning, questioning my sanity. Was last night's phone call from the doctor a dream? The following night Jean died.

I gathered my strength — isolated my feelings — phoned Pete at an out-of-state camp. In the mortuary, being with the body which had been Jean's, I experienced a different separation, a different turning point. I felt relief for him, a void for me. He was part of me and he was gone. I made the necessary arrangements for the funeral. But this was not for me. This was to carry out the beliefs and practices of society. I talked with the mortuary representative, chose a casket, talked with the rabbi. During the funeral I was there in body, my feelings in control. I was aware of the many people who had come — I talked with them. Pete was my greatest emotional support. With him I shared the loss.

After the funeral I withdrew, needing to allow myself to feel the pain of my loneliness, to experience the void. I was sad for the loss of the healthy Jean; a small part of me was still clutching at the sick Jean.

I find myself doing what he did, saying what he said, enjoying what he had enjoyed. The spirit of the delightful, capable Jean has remained with me.

I have examined my attitude toward life, death and dying. I have learned that the energy used in concern over the nature and meaning of death may be made available to cope with life's crises. Only by coming to terms with death, by accepting it as a companion, and knowing that it will eventually possess me, can I possess my life and make it richer and more meaningful.

My experience now became a source of strength. It is part of me and belongs to me. It has heightened my awareness of the shortness of life by emphasizing its quality and beauty. We tend to die the way we live. Now I feel freer, more comfortable to listen sensitively to others and help them deal with theirs.

CHAPTER 6

Psychosocial
Analysis
of
Cancer Deaths[1]

Avery D. Weisman
and
J. William Worden

Psychosocial forces have often been invoked to account for the onset and exacerbations of organic diseases [1]. Malignant illnesses have certainly not been exempted from such explorations [2]. Some investigators have asserted that certain personality traits tend to occur more frequently among patients with cancer than in comparable patients without cancer [3]. However, there are many intervening variables which must be considered, ranging from submicroscopic studies of cancer cells to epidemiological variations in cancer morbidity. One cannot disregard all other factors and simply postulate a direct connection between personality and cancer. However, modern techniques of multivariate analysis can be applied to investigate psychosocial factors found among different cancer patients without losing sight of the complexity of the cancer problem or of the individuality of the patient [4].

Statistically and biologically, some types of cancer portend a longer survival than others [5]. For example, cancer of the prostate or thyroid is compatible with a survival of many years, while cancer of the pancreas or esophagus runs a much more rapid course. With advances in radiation and

[1] This work has been supported by grants from the National Institute of Mental Health (MH15903) and the National Cancer Institute (CA14104).

chemotherapy, certain cancers once considered to be extremely fatal will have better chances of amelioration and longer survival. Among the known factors that influence the duration of life or length of survival are the histology of the tumor, its clinical and anatomical stage at diagnosis, the primary site of the lesion, the age and sex of the patient, comorbidity with other diseases, and, of course, the nature of the treatment. We should also note the influence of yet unspecified components of cancer survival and incidence which both laboratory and epidemiological studies reveal.

It is a common observation that some cancer patients with approximately identical lesions, activity, dissemination, and treatment seem to survive far longer than others who die after unexpectedly brief illnesses. Our ongoing research into psychosocial considerations of cancer patients prompted the question of whether psychosocial differences could account for any of the variance in cancer survival. Specifically, we asked if the data derived from a psychological autopsy of cancer deaths [6] could elicit differences between patients who die more quickly or more slowly than the expected survival.

Rates for cancer survival at different stages are ordinarily determined by actuarial tables [7]. These are based on large numbers of patients and information gathered from many sources. The 5-year survival has become a kind of shibboleth, measuring the effectiveness of treatment interventions [8]. Although 2- and 10-year follow-up periods are also used, prediction curves based upon actuarial projections are of limited value in deciding the plausible fate of the individual patient.

Material and Methods

In seeking various ways to study individual cancer survival, Worden, Johnston, and Harrison [9] developed a series of multiple regression equations, using material from patients who died of cancer at one of the following primary sites: Breast, Cervix, Colon, Lung, Lymphoma, and Stomach. Each regression equation contained information about the patient's age and sex, the histology of the tumor, its site and staging at diagnosis, and the treatments received during the course of illness. Statistically, both main and interaction effects were considered. Data were provided by the Massachusetts Tumor Registry, which collects information on a large number of cancer patients throughout the Commonwealth. These regression equations provide a method for generating an *Expected Survival Score* for an individual patient, given the information above.

After the expected survival score is generated, it is possible to measure how far a patient's actual survival deviated from his predicted survival, after his death. This concept, known as the *Survival Quotient* (SQ), equals the *Observed*

Survival in months, minus the *Expected Survival* in months (as generated by the regression equation) divided by the *Standard Error of Estimated Survival* in months for the normative site group on whom the expected survival regressions were built.

$$SQ = \frac{\text{Observed Survival} - \text{Expected Survival}}{\text{Standard Error of Estimate}^2}$$

The unique advantage of the SQ is its capacity to help standardize average survival times, not merely for specific forms of cancer, but across sites as well. For example, a patient with an oat cell carcinoma of the lung who survives three months longer than the expected survival is more impressive statistically than the same 3 month period would be for a patient with adenocarcinoma of the large bowel, where the expected survival is much longer. By standardizing scores for these various sites, we could then select patients from our psychological autopsy series who survived significantly longer or significantly shorter times than did the "normative" group from Tumor Registry data.

The psychological autopsy method of data collection and analysis consisted of extensive psychosocial information about 46 preterminal and terminal cancer patients, representing the six primary sites. These patients, 35 of whom died, were studied by a team of psychiatrists, psychologists, social workers, and a nurse-clinician, besides the physicians and nurses primarily responsible for care. The large number of deaths was determined by our selection criteria for the study. We sought cancer patients who might die in the foreseeable future, a period which turned out to be four weeks to one year. Data for these 35 patients were obtained from direct premortem assessment and postmortem information from survivors. Demography of these patients is shown in Table 1.

Premortem assessment and data gathering were carried out by means of open-ended interviews, social service contacts with families, nursing reports, and psychological testing. The latter included a modified TAT, sentence completion test, Cole animal test, and a Profile of Mood States (POMS). The autopsy itself collated all the information collected by the project staff and from hospital records. Psychosocial information was recorded and coded on a special research schedule, called the *Terminality/Lethality Index*. The T/L Index has three major sections: *A*—Demography, social background, and general personality traits, *S*—Suicidal ideation and behavior, and *T*—Preterminal and terminal stage information. Each major section contained many items and subsections which were also coded for computer analysis. Data from Section *S* (suicide) will be reported at a later time.

---

[2] This transforms each score into a Standard Score (z) for cross-site comparisons.

Table 1. Demography of Project Cancer Patients (deceased)   (N = 35)

		N	%
Sex:	Male	18	51
	Female	17	49
Age:	10-19	1	3
	20-29	1	3
	30-39	2	6
	40-49	6	17
	50-59	8	23
	60-69	13	37
	70-79	4	11
	80+	0	0
Race:	Caucasian	32	91
	Negro	3	9
Religion:	Catholic	23	66
	Protestant	8	23
	Jewish	4	11
Marital Status:	Single	2	6
	Married	25	71
	Widowed	3	9
	Sep/Div	5	14
Socioeconomic	I	3	9
Class:	II	1	3
	III	4	11
	IV	7	20
	V	20	57

Psychosocial information from Sections A and T were submitted to separate principal component factor analyses.[3] As a result, we found 13 factors related to A variables, and 11 factors from T variables (Tables 2 and 3). Only those factors whose Eigenvalues exceeded a criterion level of 1.00, and for whom there seemed to be significant breaks in their latent roots were included in the rotation. Factor scores were computed by the direct (non-estimation) equations outlined by Harmon [10].

Next, a Survival Quotient score was generated for each patient, and these were correlated with factor scores (Table 4). Finally, to determine the relative contribution of each factor score towards the SQ, a series of additional

[3] The data in the A factor analysis came from 86 patients—40 suicidal, 40 terminal cancer patients with no history of suicide, and 6 patients with terminal cancer and history of recent suicide. This was done to meet the broader objective of this study which has to compare lethality and terminality in suicide and cancer patients.

Table 2. Rotated Factor Loadings—Background and Personality Variables (A)

Factor I: Poor Social Relationships

44. Patient has shown lifelong inability to maintain warm mutually inter-dependent relationships	.78
36. Estimated number of friends in the vicinity	−.72
48. Clear history of mental illness	.65
38. Patient admits to trouble getting along with people	.63
47. Received psychiatric treatment prior to admission	.57
45. Has mutually destructive interdependence with another person	.50
11. Family members close, mutually supportive	−.41
46. History of rage towards himself and others	.41

Factor II: Family Separations

08. Age patient permanently left home	−.69
12. Number of family moves during childhood	.54
21. Age when first parent lost by death	−.46

Factor III: Family Deaths

29. Suicide of a relative	.73
20. Recent family deaths	.65

Factor IV: Cancer Deaths

25. Cancer death of relative	.57
22. Cancer death of mother	−.45
09. Actual or felt childhood rejection by parents	−.41
49. History of physical handicaps	.40

Factor V: Narcissistic

40. High need to control situations and others	.70
43. Excessive interest in appearance, comfort, importance, abilities	.70
41. Passively accepted situation	−.62
46. History of rage towards himself and others	.57

Factor VI: Only/Oldest Child

05. Birth Order rank	−.71
03. Number of siblings	−.67
19. Number of sibling deaths	−.51
02. Patient was foreign born	−.49
10. Destructive parent/child relationships	.47
01. Parents were foreign born	−.46

Factor VII: Early Separation

07. Childhood separation from one or both parents	.78
06. Age of childhood separation from parent/s (1-18)	.71
42. Disparity between aspirations and accomplishments	.56
50. Seriously ill in childhood	.43

Factor VIII: Unstable Family

17. Reformed alcoholic	.71
04. Step siblings	.57
15. Multi-problem family	.52

Table 2 (cont)

Factor VIII: Unstable Family (cont)

24. Cancer death of a friend	.52
10. Destructive parent/child relationships	.43
13. School difficulties (academic and behavioral)	.41

Factor IX: Life-Threatening Behavior

39. Engaged in physically dangerous activities	.69
28. Suicide of a friend	.60
18. Drug abuse	.47
21. Age when first parent lost by death	−.42

Factor X: Social Deviance

32. Number of arrests	.78
16. Heavy current alcohol use	.71
30. Number of moves in the past 5 years	.56
45. Mutually destructive relationship with another person	.44
34. Dropped all traditional religious affiliation	.41

Factor XI: Non-Participation

35. Participant in many social group activities	−.62
37. Decreased contact with friends over past year	−.59
13. School difficulties (academic and behavioral)	.54
31. Planning to move at time of illness/suicide	.40

Factor XII: Maternal Suicide

26. Suicide of mother	.67
34. Dropped traditional religious affiliation	.41
50. Seriously ill in childhood	.40

Factor XIII: Religious Change

33. Changed from family religion	.70
23. Cancer death in family	.45

Table 3. Rotated Factor Loadings—Terminal Illness Variables (T)

Factor I: Death Wish

18. Wanted to die	.85
10. Suicidal thinking	.82
13. Said didn't care if live or die (pre-terminal)	.77
14. Said didn't care if live or die (terminal)	.72
34. Conviction that he would surely die (pre-terminal)	.63
33. Most depressed late in illness	.59
32. Depression increased over course of illness	.57
29. Most anxious late in illness	.51
58. Less open with Project staff (terminal)	−.51
30. Level of depression (pre-terminal)	.49
19. Expects not to recover (pre-terminal)	.48
20. Expects not to recover (terminal)	.45
51. Considerable concern expressed regarding pain management	.40

Table 3. (cont)

Factor II: Terminal Apathy

52. Concerned about disfigurement	−.77
22. Anger about dying (pre-terminal)	−.64
23. Anger about dying (terminal)	−.52
53. Hostile towards staff and environment	−.63
04. Family expected patient to die later than he did	.48
41. Denial of symptoms and extensions of illness	.45
51. Level of concern over pain management	−.45
27. Level of anxiety (terminal)	.44

Factor III: Acceptance/Denial of Death

40. Denial of facts about illness (first order)	−.84
39. Expressed fear of death	−.83
37. Concern over long drawn out suffering (terminal)	−.75
38. Expressed fear of dying	−.72
61. Hospital staff liked the patient	.63
41. Denial of implications of illness (second order)	.56
09. In pain at time of death	.42
28. Increased anxiety over course of illness	−.40

Factor IV: Somatic Disruption

46. Higher pre-terminal symptoms and disabilities	.73
45. High symptoms and disabilities at diagnosis	.70
25. Hostility expressed towards family	.61
15. Wished to survive only under certain conditions (pre-terminal)	.60
50. Concern about disabilities (terminal)	.55
07. Patient died not alert	.40
22. Anger about dying (pre-terminal)	.40

Factor V: Survival Attitude

01. Longer medical prognosis at time of diagnosis	.83
02. Longer actual survival from diagnosis	.83
69. History of life-threatening behavior	.69
44. Acceptance of death	.63
42. Denial of impending extinction (3d order)	−.53
08. Appropriate death	.47
16. Wished to survive only under certain conditions (terminal)	.43
47. High symptoms and disabilities (terminal)	.43
56. Highly suspicious	.41

Factor VI: Terminal Closure

59. More open with Project staff over illness course	−.73
20. Expects not to recover (terminal)	.63
07. Patient died not alert	.60
05. Patient expected to die	.59
17. Patient felt illness was his fault	.51
08. Appropriate death	.43
48. Concern about disabilities (at diagnosis)	.42

Factor VII: Terminal Anxiety

26. Level of Anxiety (pre-terminal)	.83
27. Level of Anxiety (terminal)	.74

Table 3. (cont)

Factor VII: Terminal Anxiety (cont)

28. Anxiety increased over course of illness	.61
33. Most depressed late in illness	−.54
16. Wished to survive only under certain conditions (terminal)	−.48
48. Concern about disabilities (at diagnosis)	−.42

Factor VIII: No Outside Resources

64. Number of visitors while in hospital	−.87
62. Patient withdrew from others (pre-terminal)	−.75

Factor IX: Terminal Resignation

57. Less open with Project staff (pre-terminal)	.73
11. Patient was told the diagnosis	.64
12. Patient was aware of a terminal illness	.64
36. Concern over long drawn out suffering (pre-terminal)	.62
35. Conviction of certain death (terminal)	.60
17. Patient felt illness was his fault	.44

Factor X: Rising Resentment

24. Most angry late in illness	.67
31. Level of depression (terminal)	−.59
03. Lived longer than expected at diagnosis	.58
42. Denial of extinction (3d order)	−.47
43. Denial of dying	−.47
06. Staff expected patient to die later than he did	−.42
09. Pain at time of death	.42

Factor XI: Terminal Cooperation

60. Hospital staff emotionally supportive	.80
55. Lack of cooperation with hospital staff (pre-terminal)	.66
56. Lack of cooperation with hospital staff (terminal)	−.62
63. Patient withdrew from others (terminal)	−.61
47. High symptoms and disabilities (terminal)	.42
67. Family attitude toward patient-accepting (pre-terminal)	.42
68. Family attitude toward patient-accepting (terminal)	−.42
14. Didn't care if lived or died (terminal)	.41
19. Expects not to recover (pre-terminal)	.41
23. Anger about dying (terminal)	.41

multiple regression analyses were done. The A scores were regressed against SQ, and those with significance were extracted. The same was done with significant T factor scores. A final regression equation includes these factors (Table 5).[4]

Results

One demographic variable and three T factors were found to be positively correlated with survival, as determined by the SQ. The demographic variable

[4] This procedure admittedly skews the data towards maximum predictability and is based on assumptions similar to those found in step-wise regression analysis. We know that R and F are not true tests of significance. These results are not submitted as definitive but we do suggest that these are the most promising variables for future research.

Table 4. Zero Order Correlation of Demographic Variables
And Factor Scores with Survival Quotient
(N = 35)

Sex (M = 1, F = 0)		.12
Age		.06
Socio-economic class		.36[a]
Religion		
	Protestant	.03
	Catholic	-.05
	Jewish	.03
Marital Status		
	Single	.02
	Married	-.07
	Widowed	.06
	Sep/Div	.05
A Factors		
A-1	Poor social relationships	.34[a]
A-2	Family separations	-.19
A-3	Family deaths	.08
A-4	Cancer deaths	-.20
A-5	Narcissistic	-.01
A-6	First born	.07
A-7	Early separations	-.17
A-8	Unstable family	.09
A-9	Life-threatening behavior	-.00
A-10	Social deviance	.17
A-11	Non-participation	-.18
A-12	Maternal suicide	-.38[a]
A-13	Religious change	-.05
T Factors		
T-1	Death wish	-.33[a]
T-2	Terminal apathy	.40[a]
T-3	Acceptance/denial	-.35[a]
T-4	Somatic disruption	-.11
T-5	Survival attitude	-.12
T-6	Terminal closure	-.03
T-7	Terminal anxiety	.06
T-8	No outside resources	.24
T-9	Terminal resignation	-.11
T-10	Rising resentment	.38[a]
T-11	Terminal cooperation	.42[a]

[a] $p < .05$.

was the index of social position. The three T-factors were called Rising Resentment, Terminal Apathy, and Terminal Cooperation.

Table 5. Regression of Selected Variables on Survival Quotient

Variable	Coefficient	Beta weight	Partial R	t	Sig.
Socio-economic class	58.61	78.23	.75	4.53	.00
T10 Rising Resentment	36.86	39.00	.61	3.08	.01
T2 Terminal Apathy	39.65	34.35	.54	2.58	.02
T11 Terminal Cooperation	30.74	29.66	.49	2.26	.04
A2 Family Separations	−29.78	−27.87	−.44	−1.97	.07
A4 Cancer Deaths	−19.12	−24.24	−.36	−1.54	.14
T1 Death Wish	−20.11	−20.24	−.36	−1.52	.15
A1 Poor Social Relationships	−20.81	−16.00	−.27	−1.12	.28
T3 Acceptance/Denial	− 7.59	− 8.57	−.15	−0.62	.55

Intercept = −339; Standard Error = 61.6; R = .88; F = 5.41, df 10/16, p. < .01.

Two *A*- and two *T*-factors were negatively correlated with survival: Early Separation, Poor Social Relationships, Death Wish, and Acceptance/Denial of Death.[5]

Because these factors are statistical clusters of heterogeneous information (Tables 2, 3), the rubric or phrase used to name each aggregate deserves a brief characterization.

T-10. *Rising Resentment* indicates that the patient was most angry late in the illness. However, it should not be construed as necessarily indicating overt outbursts of temper. It also signifies conspicuous absence of depressive affect or of withdrawal signs in the terminal phase. The patient was well aware of impending death and demanded close attention but not to the point of alienating the staff.

T-2. *Terminal Apathy* means that patients showed so little emotion that they seemed indifferent to their plight. Because they expressed no complaints about pain, disfigurement, or even self-concern, significant others continued hoping for a reprieve.

T-11. *Terminal Cooperation* reflects a judgment by the hospital staff. Certain patients, previously called uncooperative, became more cooperative and received more support from the staff towards the end. Although in some cases families withdrew and were less accepting, the staff was more available, and interactions were more verbal.

A-2. *Early Separation* means an absence of one or both parents for extended periods during the patient's childhood and adolescence.

A-1. *Poor Social Relationships* apply to patients with long histories of having few friends, distant relationships with families, or a series of hostile but dependent associations with others.

---

[5] Factors reported here met the criteria of either a significant *t* in the regression equation or a statistically significant zero order correlation with the dependent variable. Factor A-4 was eliminated because it met neither criteria.

T-1. *Death Wish* signifies patients who are convinced that death is inevitable, want to die, or may even consider suicide. The prevailing mood is one of depression and hopelessness.

T-3. *Acceptance/Denial of Death* refers to patients who, in contrast to T-1, seem less fearful about dying, talk about it openly, with very little denial.

If we construct a composite picture, contrasting dying patients who survive longer than expected with those who succumb earlier, the following emerges:

Longer survivals are associated with patients who have good relationships with others, and manage to preserve a reasonable degree of intimacy with family and friends until the very last. They ask for and receive much medical and emotional support. As a rule, they accept the reality of serious illness, but still do not believe that death is inevitable. Hence, at times they may deny the gravity of illness or seem to repudiate the fact of becoming more feeble. They are seldom deeply depressed but may voice resentment about various aspects of their treatment and illness. Whatever anger is displayed, it should be noted, does not alienate others but commands their attention. They may be afraid of dying alone and untended, so they refuse to let others pull away without taking care of their needs.

Shorter survivals occur in patients who report poor social relationships, starting with early separations from their family of origin, and continuing throughout life. Sometimes they have had diagnosed psychiatric disorders, but almost as often talk about repeated mutually destructive relationships with people through the years. At times, they have considered suicide. Now, when treatment fails, depression deepens, and they become highly pessimistic about their progress. They want to die—a finding that often reflects more conflict than acceptance.

Discussion

This investigation has ventured into areas not previously explored systematically. There have been few precedents to use as guides [4, 11], so we have devised our own procedures.

The Survival Quotient deserves and requires repeated trials and revisions in order to demonstrate its potential value beyond its obvious limitations. In addition to limited data reported to the Registry, physical factors vary from patient to patient, even with the same disease. Treatment modalities, such as chemotherapy, cannot be regarded as if it were all the same everywhere, without allowing for different drugs, dosages, side-effects, and so forth. Even surgical treatment is apt to vary in such common disorders as cancer of the breast, where the outcome of different operations is still a moot question. Moreover, so-called normative data, gathered from large numbers of cases, do not include psychosocial information. Obviously, the larger the number of reported cases, the more diverse the psychosocial background must be. Therefore, we should assume that expected survival has a wide range of variance, due to factors still undetermined. Nevertheless, as a conceptualization, the ratio of observed to expected survival has much to recommend it, especially when the interaction with other variables is taken into consideration. The authors have already formulated an analogous quotient, called the Risk-Rescue Ratio, for the numerical evaluation of suicidal lethality [12]. Our underlying theory regards the physical components of cancer at different sites as similar to the injury inflicted during a suicidal attempt (Risk), and considers therapeutic modalities and other measurable factors as mitigating (Rescue) elements in cancer, prolonging or shortening the likelihood of recovery or remission. That is, Risk is to Rescue as Cancer is to Treatment.

We tend in our minds to combine psychosocial factors as if they were an accurate representation of an individual patient. The fact is that factor analysis, at best, is a tabulation of family traits, not a photograph depicting details in the appearance of separate family members. Differences between individual patients may not be adequately revealed in factor analysis and regression equations.

We have found that despite efforts to clarify our observations through concept definition in mutual discussion during the psychological autopsy, ambiguities inherent to ordinary language persist, and can be misleading. For example, Terminal Apathy suggests an indifference to one's plight. Rising Resentment creates an image of a patient who becomes angrier and angrier as death approaches. Although some patients do become indifferent or irate, neither phrase is quite accurate as a comprehensive descriptive term for the variables covered by that factor. Indeed, closer examination of case records shows that some patients who survived longer than expected became quite assertive about their needs, and yet were very cooperative, rather than negativistic, drawing much support from family and staff as the end drew near. While these patients were found to show Rising Resentment, they were actually able to ask for help and even give something of themselves (as long as possible) instead of withdrawing into sullen isolation.

The term "cooperative" is commonly applied to a patient who accepts and appreciates whatever help can be given, without demanding more than is possible. Obviously, patients with longstanding habits of personal isolation may alienate themselves from others, be considered "uncooperative," and be cut off from available help, thereby perpetuating a tragic cycle of need, negative feelings, deprivation, and further needs. Nevertheless, regardless of this "existential despair," and other individual variations, these "negatively perceived" patients had statistically shorter survivals. In some instances, depression and a wish for death may be secondary to an unfortunate breakdown in care-taking hospital functions, induced by a patient with an objectionable attitude and unappreciative manner. We should also recognize that an alert and compassionate staff might learn to identify irritating patients, and to tolerate certain kinds of hostile behavior. Otherwise, the staff may fail to provide necessary care and support, and, statistically at least, shorten the patient's life. Few patients die by themselves, alone and uncared for. The quality of care, however, differs enormously, even within the same hospital, on different services, and even from shift to shift. Duff and Hollingshead [13] have eloquently documented discrepancies in diagnosis, treatment, and communication found among doctors and patients with approximately the same disease.

Other studies [14, 15, 16] have shown that the presence or absence of significant denial in the terminal phase is seldom a decisive issue by itself. Denial appears in varying forms at different stages of illness, just as there are different types of death anxiety. Denial and acceptance of death are present together, but their equilibrium and proportions shift in response to a patient's perception of the diagnosis, treatment procedures, prognosis, significant relationships, and communications with others [17]. A patient who fails to speak out may do so for many reasons. The family and staff can interpret the patient's silence as indifference, depression, contentment, lack of awareness, resignation, or even as a sign of mental dissolution.

Patients who survived longer did not complain about pain or at least excessive discomfort. This finding may indicate better pain control through medication, but sufficient medication itself may be a sign of better general care. Furthermore, although we cannot exclude those cases in which cancer has invaded nerve roots and caused intractable pain, poorly controlled pain may indicate inadequate total care, a situation which can lead to irritability, despair, fatigue, manifold complaints, and a more serious outlook.

These caveats are intended to show how carefully we must interpret clinical behavior, because our judgments may influence how we rate patients with respect to different variables. This, in turn, will influence any factor analysis. Even though our clinical judgments are at times open to scrutiny, in contrast, the literature of thanatology is replete with unsubstantiated generalities which often sound more homiletic than scientific. Detailed instructions about how to intervene with different kinds of patients are usually lacking, except for admonitions about the dignity of death. Clinical and statistical psychosocial analysis is arduous, especially when one considers how exhausting and emotionally depleting the care of dying patients can be. Nevertheless, appropriate research methods and normative information are prerequisites for psychosocial management of terminal cancer [18]. Otherwise, thanatologists will shortly find themselves embedded in platitudes and bathos, unable to move effectively for lack of structured information and useful instruments. For these reasons, even relatively crude procedures with obvious shortcomings can be the impetus for further scientific investigations.

Conclusions

1. Psychosocial analysis of the dying process can be systematically carried out for both individual patients and for different kinds of cancer deaths. The Survival Quotient is an important tool in this task, because it compares observed survival with expected survival, and it can make comparison possible between different forms of cancer with varying prognoses.

2. In general, we found that longevity—as a statistical entity in cancer deaths—was significantly correlated with patients who could maintain active and mutually responsive relationships, provided that the intensity of demands was not so extreme as to alienate the people responsible for the patient's care.

3. In contrast, shorter survival was found among cancer patients who reflected longstanding alienation, deprivation, depression, and destructive relationships, which extended into the terminal stage of life. These attitudes of patients were expressed in despondency, desire to die, contemplation of suicide, inordinate complaints, all of which heaped more self-defeat and isolation upon themselves.

4. Closer attention to individual factors among dying patients could lead health professionals to more appropriate and no less compassionate interventions. Better understanding of dying patients as people with unique personalities and different requirements for reciprocal communication may result in devising strategies for coping with death that conceivably could extend, or at least improve cancer survival.

ACKNOWLEDGMENT

We wish to acknowledge and thank Frederick G. Guggenheim, M.D., Harry S. Olin, M.D., Joe P. Lemon, M.S.W., Mary Vallier, R.N., Robert Sterling-Smith, Ph.D., and Lee C. Johnston, M.A. for their assistance in the collection of these data. An earlier version of this paper was prepared for the conference on "Death Research: Methods and Substance," Berkeley, California, March 21-23, 1973.

REFERENCES

1. Wolff, H., Wolf, S., and Hare, C. (Eds.). *Life Stress and Bodily Disease.* Baltimore: The Williams and Wilkins Company, 1950.
2. Holland, J. "Psychologic Aspects of Cancer." *Cancer Medicine.* J. Holland and E. Frei (eds.). Philadelphia: Lea and Febiger, Ch. XVI-2, 991-1021.

3. Bahnson, C. and Kissen, D. (Eds.). *Psychophysiological Aspects of Cancer.* New York: Annals of New York Academy of Sciences, 1966: 125, 733-1055. Also, Bahnson, E., (Ed.). Second Conference in Psychophysiological Aspects of Cancer. New York: Annals of New York Academy of Sciences, 1969: 164, 307-634.

4. Achte, K., Vauhkonen, M., and Viitamaki, O. Part I: "Psychic Factors in Cancer." Part II: "Psychological Determinants of Cancer." *Cancer and Psyche.* Monographs from the Psychiatric Clinic of the Helsinki University Central Hospital, 1(1970).

5. Silverberg, E. and Holleb, A. "Cancer Statistics, 1974—Worldwide Epidemiology." *Ca—A Cancer Journal for Clinicians,* 1974: 24(1), 2-21.

6. Weisman, A. D. *The Realization of Death: A Guide for the Psychological Autopsy.* New York: Jason Aronson, Inc., 1974.

7. National Cancer Institute. *End Results in Cancer: Report No. 3.* Bethesda, Maryland: Department of Health, Education, and Welfare, 1968.

8. James, A. Cancer Prognosis Manual, American Cancer Society Publication, 1966.

9. Worden, J. W., Johnston, L., and Harrison, R. "Survival Quotient as a Method for Psychosocial Investigation of Cancer Death." *Psychological Reports* (in press).

10. Harmon, H.H.: *Modern Factor Analysis.* Chicago, University of Chicago, Press, 1967.

11. Kastenbaum, R. and Aisenberg, R. *The Psychology of Death.* New York: Springer Publishing Co. Inc., 1972.

12. Weisman, A. D. and Worden, J. W. "Risk-Rescue Rating in Suicide Assessment." *Archives of General Psychiatry,* 1972: 26, 553-560.

13. Duff, R. and Hollingshead, A. *Sickness and Society.* New York, Evanston and London: Harper and Row, 1968.

14. Keltikangas-Jarvinen, L. "Attitudes Toward Death—An Empirical Study with Normal and Psychiatrically Disturbed Persons." Yearbook of the Psychiatric Clinic of Helsinki University Central Hospital, 1971, 161-165.

15. Imboden, J. "Psychosocial Determinants of Recovery." *Psychosocial Aspects of Physical Illness,* Z. Lipowski (Ed.) S. Karger, Basel, 1972:8, 142-155.

16. Hinton, J. *Dying.* Baltimore: Penguin Books, 1967.

17. Weisman, A. D. *On Dying and Denying: A Psychiatric Study of Terminality.* New York: Behavioral Publications, 1972.

18. Weisman, A. "Psychosocial Considerations in Terminal Care." *Psychosocial Aspects of Terminal Care,* Schoenberg, B., Carr, A., Peretz, D. and Kutscher, A. (Eds.). New York and London: Columbia University Press, 1972.

PART 2
Meanings of Death

Death is the end and the end result of the dying process. Its meanings are numerous, and its significance is immense, both to the individual who is dying and to other persons in that individual's milieu. In some ways, reading paragraphs like this one about death tend to remove some of the power and vitality that inheres in death; we weaken it by talking or writing or reading about it. Be alert to not permitting your academic exercises with death to dull your sensitivity to death's emotional impact.

The first two chapters look directly at meanings. Marcovitz offers an overview, covering a number of death-related issues; Sheskin and Wallace describe the meanings of losing a husband through various kinds of death, since even in death, a status system exists; Pine broadens the background by discussing death in a general social framework. Thus, these three chapters move from the dying/dead person to the family members to the general community.

The next three chapters back up a step. Kastenbaum and Briscoe study people in their native habitat: the urban street. They look at death as something we risk each moment, and some take more risks than others. Marshall describes older people who are both ready to live and ready to die, pointing out that those who want to live want to live *for* something. And Saul and Saul present a transcript of older persons as they talk, most heatedly, about the right to die. Judging from this article, the elderly discuss the same issues in the same ways as younger people, and they end up with the same wisdom, the same confusion, and the same inability to resolve the conflict.

What, then, is the meaning of death? You need to answer that for yourself, but hopefully this section will provide you with a better understanding of some of the issues and with some knowledge of how others view the meaning of death. After all, the only reason you may want a "final" answer to the question is to reduce your own anxieties, and there are times when it is appropriate to be anxious.

What Is the
Meaning of Death
to the Dying Person
and His Survivors?

Eli Marcovitz

A death in the family affects the survivors both as individuals and as members of a group. Although both aspects are important, this paper limits itself to a discussion of some of the great variety of effects on the individuals involved.

SOME MEANINGS OF DEATH

What is the meaning of death? We have libraries of eschatology devoted to that question. But the fundamental question about the meaning of death is not that raised by philosophers, theologians, biologists, or psychologists. It is the question asked, even though not verbalized, by the child when he first becomes aware that he himself eventually will die. It is not, "What is the meaning, significance or purpose of death," but rather: "Why do I have to die?" That question probably remains somewhere in the mind of every human being until he dies.

Unless they have had lives of chronic deprivation or suffering, children tend to take gratification for granted. For any trauma, however, the mother is held responsible. Throughout life we tend to continue this pattern, to blame outside forces for our suffering. These are either malevolent forces which hurt us unjustly, or forces representing the Good or God, which should mete out only deserved punishment.

Cassirer [1] proposed that "The conception that man is mortal, by his nature and essence, seems to be entirely alien to mythical and primitive religious thought." Perhaps this is also true for children, as well as for the child which each of us carries within himself. From a psychoanalytic perspective, in our unconscious, irrational mental processes, death is never conceived as a natural process. It always means being killed. It takes experience and wisdom to know one's own responsibility and the role of impersonal, uncontrollable forces. Living is not questioned, it is accepted as a given. Dying is felt to be a deprivation, a punishment.

What does death deprive us of? Every moment of living is accompanied by some degree of affect, along the spectrum of mild pleasure to ecstasy or along the spectrum of displeasure to unbearable pain. Unless it is specifically painful, every sensation, every movement, every thought is accompanied by pleasure. It is possible that all brain activity, unless it involves the stimulation of specific pain areas, has some reverberation into the so-called reward or pleasure areas which are deep within the base of the brain, and that this process provides the biological basis for our love of life. In this sense it can be said "pleasure is the absence of pain." Death deprives us of this pleasure of living. It also deprives us of our relationship with people, relationships in which we have experienced loving and being loved, and in which we have given or received security and help, and which have contributed to our feelings of worth and to our sense of identity and of belonging.

But death is not only a deprivation, it is a threat, a punishment. It is not surprising that, on becoming aware of one's impending death, the reaction is so frequently, "why me?" This cry is in effect a protest against injustice, meaning "I have done nothing to deserve this punishment."

On many occasions, when patients have talked of death with fear or with longing, I have asked what it means to them. Usually the answer is that it is the end of living, it is nothingness. Sometimes I hear a more sophisticated intellectual answer, that death is a part of life, or that dying is a part of living. Frequently it is said that it is not death which is feared but the painful process of dying, not only the physical pain, but the separation from the living, the envy of the living, the relegation to the periphery, the loneliness, the restriction of power and mobility, the dependence, the indignity so frequent in the process of dying. Yet, at the same time that people deny the fear of death, it invariably becomes evident that they both fear and long for it—and still do not believe in it! Death always includes the fantasy, conscious or unconscious, of some kind of continuation of existence in some other mode.

We have many ways of dealing with the fear of death. Some people consciously repudiate the idea that death is an inevitable end to life, with the certainty that scientific advances will enable humans to live indefinitely. Many religions proclaim that what is called death is a transition to another form of existence. This may be in the form of reincarnation or transmigration of the soul into another body, human or animal, or by way of the immortality of the soul, or even by reaching through some form of meditation or ordeal the highest levels of *satori* beyond those levels from which one can still return. In this approach death is merely an ASC, an Altered State of Consciousness, the most beautiful, ineffable state of being, of union with the infinite.

This attitude is illustrated in the best-seller, "Jonathan Livingston Seagull" [2]. In this little story, a seagull rejects the ordinary seagull's life of food-seeking, to become the supreme flyer, finding ecstasy in new ways of flight to heights and depths and speeds never reached before. At one point, he crashes into a cliff to what would ordinarily be death. Two gulls who are evidently angel-gulls come and lift him to immortal flight. Apparently this story embodies the fantasies of a considerable number of our young people.

It can be maintained that the universality of the conscious or unconscious belief in some form of continued existence after death is evidence of its truth or reality, a truth beyond the reach of logic, of rationality, or scientific validation. We know also that we are capable of believing anything we want to believe and denying anything we want to deny, regardless of the evidence or lack of it. Especially in the face of death, the rational tends to give way to the irrational.

Sometimes an awareness of impending death precipitates a euphoric reaction. This is the ideally-hoped-for response for the devout religious person who anticipates a life after death in a union with God. I do not know how frequently the euphoric reaction actually occurs in such situations. This state is similar to those described as religious ecstasy or to the ecstatic experiences attained by some users of hallucinogens or by some practitioners of certain forms of meditation. Although this euphoria has its roots in the earliest undifferentiated state of oneness of mother and infant, it may be simplistic reductionism to attempt to understand such complex human experiences solely in terms of their most primitive origins. In any case, this ultimate happiness fulfills the fantasy of the attainment of all desire and of all ideals, and the freedom from all conflict, disappointment, and pain. It embodies omnipotence, omniscience, and immortality—man's universal dream of para-dise. There are some, the dare-devils, whose life theme seems to be a counterphobic attempt to master the fear of death by gambling with it, challenging it, repeatedly risking it. This may be in the form of dangerous sports, reckless driving, the acceptance of dares, the use of dangerous drugs, or in the readiness to face dangers in the service of various political, religious or moral causes. Some degree of this is a normal characteristic of adolescence, and may be part of the formal "rites of passage" into manhood.

Identification With Death

There is another method that people use to master the fear of death [3]. I call it "identification with death," modelled on the defense-mechanism of "identification with the aggressor." Soldiers must be taught to become killers, not only to become effective warriors, but to diminish their own fears of being killed. One way to master the fear of death is to become oneself an embodiment of some figure or representative of death.

Some time ago, in a TV film about wolves, a hunter was seen "wolfing" down the raw flesh of a wolf he had just killed. Wolves, like all beasts of prey, are killers, symbols of death. To eat the flesh of a wolf is to become like it, a killer, a master of death. In the bull-fight the bull, the totem-animal, in addition to symbolizing the father, also is death, which the hero must face and conquer. The "moment of truth," when the matador faces the bull and performs the final thrust, is the "moment of ecstasy" when matador and bull become one. This is one of the most dramatic examples of identification with death as a means of mastering its terror.

Another example is Captain Ahab's final union with Moby Dick, the white whale, the killer, which, among other meanings, also represented death.

These examples which illustrate the process of "identification with death" all involve traditionally masculine roles, i.e., the hunter or warrior. Is there any comparable feminine way of mastering the fear of death? In the history of mankind it was in the battle or the hunt that men actively faced their greatest threats as men. Women faced their greatest dangers as women in pregnancy and childbirth. I should guess that it is in the delivery of a child, in becoming the giver of life, that the woman masters her fear of death.

Picasso's famous sculpture, "The Death's Head," was done during the year he was expecting to die in accordance with a prediction made by a friend many years before. There is a photo of Picasso with a striking look of triumph, holding this immense bronze head. For the gifted ones who have the potential to deal in some creative fashion with the threat of death this is the most effective form of mastery.

To Be Devoured

There is another component to the terror of death, which I believe is deeply unconscious and seldom expressed in words. To die means to be devoured. This unconscious expectation rests on a number of sources. Animals die and are eaten by other animals. From the time that our ancestors were able to foresee their own inevitable death, they developed rituals and practices of burial designed to ensure protection against being devoured. Human cannibalism, actual or token or ritual and symbolic, has been part of the history of most human societies. Not least among the sources of this terror is the unconscious expectation of retaliatory punishment for the universal cannibalistic wishes and fantasies of childhood. In myths and legends are records of this terror. The saviour-hero conquers death, the devouring monster, the dragon or the minotaur. Death itself is represented as the skeleton from which the flesh and organs have been removed and eaten. Death and the victim are the same. And what of our ritual funeral feasts? What is being eaten? One of its meanings is the flesh of the deceased. I believe this fear of being devoured is one of the reasons for the fear of dying alone, away from family and friends, unprotected from the predator.

Yet there are things that are worse than death.

This is Emily Dickinson:

> Suspense is hostiler than Death.
> Death, though soever broad,
> Is just Death, and cannot increase.
> Suspense does not conclude,
> But perishes to live anew,
> But just anew to die,
> Annihilation plated fresh
> With immortality.

Intractable pain, anxiety, despair, hopelessness, the pain of melancholia, for these death is a relief.

Heaven, Hell, And Death

Recently some of us had the opportunity to see a film of episodes in the last year in the life of a boy of eleven, who was living and dying with leukemia. Toward the end, he asks his father, "What is heaven like?" Consideration of this episode was part of the discussion which followed the film. It was not surprising that hell was not mentioned in the film. I was a little surprised that no one, not even the theologians present, mentioned hell in our discussion. Of course, the idea of hell is not fashionable just now, but even though it may be repressed or denied, the fear of hell is just as ubiquitous as the hope of heaven. Recently a young woman from a non-religious family talked of her childhood images of death, of heaven and of hell, and her fears of having to suffer eternally in hell.

Besides the hope of infinite reward, death also includes the anticipation of future punishment, in the forms of an eternity of suffering and of eternal frustration of all desire. In Dante, the frustration of Tantalus represents this component of hell. Tortured by thirst, he stands to his chin in a pool of water, but the instant he lowers his head to drink the water vanishes. Trees bow their branches offering fruit but when he raises his arms the winds whirl them out of reach.

I am quite sure that the boy in the film who knew the promise of heaven also knew the threat of hell, and felt it as threatened punishment. By the time a child conceptualizes catastrophe, it is impossible to separate it from punishment.

I am certain that the comfort of the Last Rites depends as much on the absolution of sin as on the attainment of grace. I remember a young man in analysis who was in the process of discarding his religious practices. Yet on

Yom Kippur he found himself attending services and fasting all day. He asked himself "why?" and was surprised by the recognition that an important purpose was insurance: a day of relatively minor discomfort might reduce the chance of an eternity of punishment.

A young woman has made repeated suicidal attempts at times when she becomes terrified of being tortured and killed.[1] It is not only that suicide will save her from death by torture. It appears that, for her, self-inflicted death means a peaceful union with God and Mother in heaven while death at the hand of the torturer will lead to hell. Obviously, since it leads to hell, the death by torture must deserve eternal punishment. I think it can be hypothesized that the masochistic fantasy must be her version of the incestous wish, and this is why it leads to hell. Certainly, this is undoubtedly only one component of meaning in a complicated set of fantasies, but it serves to illustrate the point that death includes fantasies of heaven and hell, of rewards and punishments.

I believe that in the rituals attending dying, whether they be the formalized rituals of religion or the informal ones of family and friends, some form of amulet against hell may help to reduce the terror. The assurance, "You are loved and forgiven" should accompany the assurance of immortality, "You will remain in our memory and in the memory of our children forever."

I wonder if, besides relief of physical suffering and protection against indignity and demoralization, these are not the most precious gifts we can offer to the dying person. To be effective, these assurances must be communicated in action as well as in words. This means that the family behaves with love and care and expresses its closeness and support through the entire process of dying. But here is the difficulty: members of the family do not always have or maintain such feelings, nor do they know always when a person is dying.

Meanings of Death to the Survivors

Many factors combine to determine the feelings and reactions that accompany the experience of a death in the family. There are spontaneous reactions, emotions, thoughts, and actions which are inevitably modified by considerations regarding the expected and proper. The spontaneous reactions may include somatic components, cardiovascular, gastrointestinal or even loss of consciousness.

Obvious variables affecting the reactions are the relationship and relative ages of the dying person and the survivor, as well as the complicated states of feelings that existed between them throughout their lives. The death of a child produces different effects, depending on whether it is a young child or

[1] I am indebted to Dr. Melvin Singer for this illustration of the equation of death with heaven and hell.

whether the child is already a parent or even a grandparent. It makes a difference which child, or whether it is an only child or one of a large number of siblings. The loss of sibling, spouse, parent, grandparent, all have different effects. Even the loss of an uncle, aunt or cousin may have significant effects depending on the nature and degree of closeness of feelings. Perhaps, the most important elements depend on the specific relationship, the meaning of the person, the functions of the dead person in the life of the survivor and the nature of the changes that ensue from the death.

The survivor may be aware of many of these, but usually not of all. Surprise at one's own emotions and behavior is not unusual. The surprise may be at the quality of feeling, or at its intensity or even at the lack of feeling. Of course, depending on one's control and on considerations of propriety, the actual feelings may have little relationship to the behavior that can be observed by others.

I find it extremely difficult to make valid generalizations about the reactions of survivors to the death of someone in the family. We might approach consideration of the effects from one of the fundamental organizing principles of human behavior—narcissism. "How does this event affect my life immediately and in the future?" Regardless of the degree to which one is aware of it, this consideration is important in everyone's reactions.

On hearing that his child was run over by a car a father cries out, "Why did this have to happen to me?" Obviously this man has a great deal of narcissism, else he might have asked why this had to happen to the child. Yet, any threat or trauma tends to bring out narcissistic responses. When it doesn't, we call it heroism. So, when death threatens or hits close, we must expect a tendency to a narcissistic response. In the death of others we look for signs affecting ourselves. In obituary columns why is the age of the deceased always in the first paragraph, if not actually in the headline? Because there is the universal game "How many more years does this give me? or "By how many years have I already exceeded him?" In the family, where the threat is closest, the tendency to a narcissistic reaction is the strongest. Declarations tend to start from the self. "I suffer most," or "I must have my share," or "I am innocent. I have done all that could possibly have been expected," or "I am guilty, I could have done more." Each person's reaction has its narcissistic component.

Guilt reactions are likely to cause serious disturbances. It is so usual to find people suffering from guilt because of wishes for the death of someone whose existence is an unending drain, whether for need of money, or time, or attention, or physical care, or for any other reason. This is especially true toward the old or chronically ill. The feeling of guilt means "I am inconsiderate, ungrateful, hateful, evil, to have such wishes." If the person is not neurotically bound to belief in the omnipotence of thought, i.e., the conviction that the wish is the equivalent of the deed, or that the wish will cause the death, then it has frequently been helpful to describe a classical experiment in biology: a frog is pithed, that is, an instrument is inserted between the base of the skull and the upper end of the spine and the spinal cord is severed from the brain. The frog is fastened upright to a board and it hangs limp and paralyzed. A bit of absorbent cotton is dipped in acid and applied to the side of the lower back. Very soon the hind leg lifts up against the force of gravity and brushes off the offending object. This illustrates a basic principle of living matter: it attempts to free itself from a distressing stimulus. To *wish* for freedom from a burden is part of our biological makeup, it is neither good nor evil. Only our *deeds* warrant judgment. It is usually a relief to realize that such wishes are natural and universal, and that one is not condemned as a criminal for having them. It is what one does about wishes that characterizes the person in terms of good and evil.

Guilt for such death-wishes can occur only in a person who also loves the one who is dying. The feeling of guilt always indicates a hurtful wish or deed toward someone who is loved or who is felt to deserve love or loyalty. In Hawthorne's Dr. *Rappacini's Daughter*, the doctor says, "Blessed are all single emotions, be they dark or light. It is the lurid admixture of the two that brings on the fires of the infernal regions." It is always the experience of complicated or contradictory feelings that gives us trouble. This is usually the situation in relation to the dying or to the death of someone in the family.

Death wishes toward the dying are not the only cause of guilt. A mother lost her first child from a congenital malformation which was discovered only after the mother became pregnant with the next child. Twenty years later she still felt guilty, from the idea that if she had not been so anxious to have a second child, she would not have been pregnant during the illness of the first child and would have had more time and energy to care for the sick child more adequately and perhaps it would not have died. But even more guilt was due to the abortion of her first pregnancy some years earlier because at the time her future husband had not considered marriage, and persuaded her to have the abortion. She could not get rid of the conviction that she had been punished for the abortion by losing her first-born.

For a young child, besides the expected anxiety at being left unprotected in a dangerous world, the loss of a parent is frequently felt as a punishment for death-wishes against the parent, a punishment on the order of King Midas' punishment: the fulfillment of a sinful wish simultaneously constitutes its punishment. To the child's limited understanding, to be told that a parent has gone to heaven, a place of joy, must necessarily mean having been abandoned. And how many children have heard the cry, "You'll be the death of me." When it happens the child cannot help feeling responsible. If the child were told the truth of death, even within the limits of his understanding, he could probably face better the loss with less feeling of his responsibility for it. Yet, one could immediately ask, "Who is to determine what shall be taught as the truth of death?"

For adults, the loss of a child or of a spouse may be experienced as punishment. When the punishment is felt to be deserved the reaction is frequently guilt and depression. Or the punishment may be considered to be proof of guilt if one believes that under God only the guilty are punished. Such reactions of guilt and depression may lead to somatic illness, self-injury or suicide. Sometimes, any of these may occur as "anniversary reactions" at later times.

When the punishment is felt to be undeserved, then the reaction is anger at someone who is considered responsible. Remember, unconsciously a death is always a killing. Someone is to blame: God or fate or the physician or someone else in the family. I used to be surprised at how frequently I found people to be unaware that they believed in a personal God who intervened in their lives. This belief often was revealed by their reaction of anger at the occurrence of some misfortune, especially a death. But they never knew what or whom they were angry at. Frequently, it was in the form of a spontaneous denial that they revealed that their anger was at God. Either they denied a belief in God, or denied that their concept of God included His interest in and control of their lives and that His interventions were based on justice and fairness. Usually they recalled that in childhood they used to believe such notions, and only reluctantly were they able to see how much their current emotional reactions contradicted their proclaimed rationality. In any case, the greater one's need to deny one's own guilt, the greater the need for a scapegoat to carry the blame. This process can be most devastating between husband and wife when each blames the other for the death of a child.

It is so frequently deplored that the dying person is written off, abandoned. There are many reasons for this. The ones who will go on living feel embarrassment at their triumph and sometimes resentment at the envy and anger expressed by the one who is soon to die. Only rarely can the dying person really express humor. A granduncle of mine, near death, was visited by his physician, who said on leaving, "I'll see you tomorrow." The reply was "Thank you, but will I see you?" In the realm of unconscious fantasy, death *is* catching, through the unconscious process of introjection. People have a horror of touching or kissing a dying person or a corpse. It is feared that, by visual, tactile, oral or respiratory introjection, identification with the dying person will take place and both will die.

There is also anger at the dead. How frequent are such recriminations: "Why didn't he take care of himself?" "Why did he do all the things he wasn't supposed to do?" The implication is that he was not considerate of his wife and children.

The hatred here is for the betrayal. "If he loved us as he should have he would not have died and left us this way." Sometimes this complaint is justified. It occurs in many circumstances, e.g., when a man fails to leave a will, or allows insurance to lapse, or denies that he has a fatal illness and neglects practical details that affect significantly the welfare of his family. But the situation is sometimes complicated by the fact that the wife has been tortured by her inability to speak frankly about such matters for fear of distressing her husband by forcing him to face his approaching death. This reluctance to speak of such things is partly out of love and partly out of a fear of appearing hostile or greedy. Also there is the fear of magic, putting a thought into words gives it substance. If the wish is present then there is more likely to be evasion, euphemism or crude attack.

Besides narcissistic reactions, death wishes, hatreds, guilt, avarice, relief, etc., death and dying bring out loving feelings. Respect, affection, appreciation, love, may reach expression in direct ways that may not have been possible before. Such emotions may be between the dying person and members of the family, or they may come out among the family members to each other. Sometimes the loss of one person in a group makes each of the survivors more precious to each other. This can lead to new levels of close relationship in the group.

On the other hand, the death of a key figure who has been the hub of a family can lead to its disintegration, with virtual alienation of each from the others. This is especially true when members of the family have been hostile to each other or have been geographically dispersed. When adult children are the survivors and have their own families and lives, then the loss of the key figure, father or mother usually, causes no great disruption in their lives. It is when the immediate survivors include young children that the death may be seriously disorganizing. The degree of the trauma and disorganization depends chiefly on the effectiveness, integrity, resources, and motivations of the surviving parent and, to a lesser degree, on these same factors in the children.

A great deal has been written about normal reactions of grief and mourning which most people feel at the loss of someone who has been loved. The duration and intensity of such reactions vary tremendously and one cannot tell from manifest behavior what is being experienced subjectively. Much depends on the character of the person and the nature of the relationship. The bereft person usually feels sadness and loss, but is able to go through the "work of mourning" to an acceptance of the separation. The variations in this process depend to a large extent on the nature of earlier experiences of separation and loss. What were the ages at which the previous experiences occurred? Was there someone who was a more or less satisfactory substitute for the lost love object at the time? Was the person able to react to the loss in a way that contributed to a maturing process or were the conditions such that he tended to regress or become fixated in ways which interfered with the normal developmental process?

The pathological reaction of depression differs qualitatively from normal grief. Here there is a much greater element of guilt and ambivalence. The hurt is not so much at the loss of a loved object as it is a reaction of injured narcissism. It is this that makes the depressive reaction so painful, protacted, and full of hatred.

This reaction depends on there having been a narcissistic relationship with the deceased person. By this, I mean a relationship in which the other person is experienced as part of oneself. The other person's purpose in living is conceived as devoted to the enhancement or service of oneself. It is in such cases that the loss is felt as rejection, abandonment, betrayal. One wants revenge and has no object, only memories to direct the hatred against. This turns into self hatred, feelings of impotence and worthlessness and may lead to suicide.

Helping Survivors to Reintegrate

The problem of remarriage after the death of the spouse can be a distressing one. It is common to hear adverse judgments on people who remarry without waiting for what is considered to be a socially proper period of mourning. The accusation is that this is proof that there was not sufficient love for the spouse. The time of remarriage is certainly no criterion of the nature of the relationship in the original marriage. Such social judgments only reflect the bias of the observer.

People vary in the degree of fluidity or rigidity which characterizes their relationships to loved objects. A relationship that is meaningful and important may feel unique, so that it is inconceivable that any other could ever replace it. One might feel disloyal, a betrayer, to love anyone else. On the other hand, the worship of the memory of a lost love may be a way of avoiding the less-than-ideal realities of any new love. Usually after a process of psychological separation, which varies for every person, there is a readiness to form a new relationship.

There are people who have the capacity to go from one relationship to another with little distress or meaning. Usually this is a manifestation of superego pathology related to disturbance in early relationships, particularly to the mother. On the other hand, such fluidity may represent a terrible need for attachment which makes unendurable any period of separation or aloneness. For me it is not helpful in understanding such varieties of relationship to think in terms of flow of libidinal or aggressive energy between the self and the object. Such a concept represents only a more abstract level of description. One really has to know a person's whole history of relationship to loved objects to understand the significance of any specific instance. Outsiders are in no position to judge.

How can we help families to reintegrate after traumatic disruptions, and to lessen the traumatic effects of such disruptions? There is increasing interest and concern with the effects of new aspects of these phenomena: dying in institutions instead of at home, dying alone instead of in the presence of the family modern medicine's prolongation of living and of dying, the isolation and fragmentation of families in our society, the increasing dependence on various kinds of agencies in the community instead of on the family. All these changes in our living and dying force re-evaluation of attitudes and practices which may no longer be as appropriate as they were in the past.

First of all, I think we must recognize that no matter how much we may feel that earlier modes were better, there is no going back. We cannot restore a Golden Age that actually never was, but exists only in our fantasies. Today's children will probably know death only as the result of violence, and seldom experience it directly as the natural final process of living. That kind of death occurs in hospitals and in nursing or old age homes where children rarely are encouraged to enter.

Can we replace such direct experience with educational measures that will enable children to know death, to feel, think, and fantasy about the death of people important to them and about their own inevitable death in ways which might reduce the distortions, the terrifying irrationality, the unnecessary aspects of the experiences of guilt, hurt, hatred of others and of themselves which are so frequently components of experience with death? Granted that rational knowledge is of some help in the struggle with the irrational, I still have some doubts that educational methods alone would have much effect. I can't forget a brilliant student at one of the foremost colleges in the area who was getting an A in her course in Astronomy and at the same time believed so strongly in Astrology that she had to know the birthday of a young man before she would date him.

Throughout the history of humankind most people have depended on the irrational in their dealing with death and dying. Many forms of magic are designed to deal with death, in effect to confer immortality. In the tenets of religion one can find support for the idea of a life after death, or for the idea that death is all and there is no hereafter, sometimes both in the same religion.

If one believes the former, then it is possible to maintain that for the dying person and the surviving family nothing else matters but preparation for an afterlife, and all our talk here is ridiculous. If one believes the latter, then one is more likely to try to make the experience of death and dying part of a more fulfilling experience of living. Others can say it is possible to do both, to reduce the suffering of this life and to prepare for an afterlife as well. In the end people follow their own bent and act and believe as they need to and wish to.

In closing, I must refer to a relatively recent problem for both the dying person and the survivors—that is, the matter of the prolongation of the process of living and dying, when everyone knows that there is no hope of recovery or of freedom from pain or indignity. This problem raises many difficult points, medical, ethical, religious, psychological, and economic. I have no answer, but I should like to leave you with another poem by Emily Dickinson.

> The heart asks pleasure first
> And then, excuse from pain,
> And then, those little anodynes
> That deaden suffering,
> And then, to go to sleep,
> And then, if it should be
> The will of its Inquisitor
> The liberty to die.

REFERENCES

1. Cassirer, E. *An essay on man*. NY: Doubleday & Co., 1953.
2. Bach, R. *Jonathon Livingstone Seagull*. NY: Avon, 1973.
3. Marcovitz, E. Man in search of meaning—hallucinogenic agents. *Bull. Philadelphia Assoc. for Pennsylvania*, 1970, 20, 171-195.

CHAPTER
8

Differing Bereavements:
Suicide, Natural,
and Accidental Death

Arlene Sheskin
and
Samuel E. Wallace

Two recently published works, *After Suicide* by Samuel E. Wallace [1] and *The First Year of Bereavement* by Ira O. Glick, Robert S. Weiss, and C. Murray Parkes [2], provide an opportunity to explore the way in which bereavement experiences are shaped by differences in cause of death, and/or by anticipation of death. Wallace examined bereavement reactions from suicide, while Glick, Weiss, and Parkes were concerned with bereavement which follows natural death and accidents.

Both studies were longitudinal in nature. The Glick study was done from 1965 to 1969, the Wallace study from 1970 to 1971. In both projects bereaved persons were contacted via death certificates registered in the Boston Metropolitan Area. All were widows, their age range from nineteen to sixty-two. The social class characteristics of respondents in these samples are also similar. Both samples are composed of working and middle class respondents. Their respective racial distribution, however, is quite dissimilar. The suicide widows are all white [1], while the natural and accidental death widows were 24 per cent black [2]. Racial composition is thus the greatest difference in these two studies.

The mode of analysis invoked in these studies also facilitates comparison. Following the *verstehen* approach to social life with primarily descriptive statistics, these authors engaged in intensive interviewing in order to gain an understanding of their respondent's experiences. Wallace and his associates met with each of the twelve widows in his sample almost monthly over the period of a year for interviews that ranged from two to four hours each. Glick, Weiss and Parkes met three times with each of their forty-eight widows also for open-ended intensive interview.

While these similarities in the two studies do not yield matched groups, they do allow the presumption that there are some similarities in the social worlds of these respondents. Similar though their two samples may be, neither study is representative of the entire universe of bereaved persons and care must be exercised in drawing conclusions from their respective findings.

Having noted the similarities and differences in these two publications, the observations which stem from our comparison of their findings can be presented in these general areas: anticipation of death; personal reactions; reactions of others to the death; adjustment and re-involvement; and future bereavement research.

Anticipation

Anticipation is an important element in a widow's ability to accept the death of her spouse regardless of cause of death is a finding upon which both studies concur. Glick notes that 21 per cent of the widows in his sample lost their husbands without warning through accidents or natural death, 23 per cent knew their husbands were ill but did not expect their death; for the remaining widows (56%), the spouse's death culminated a long illness.

While Glick, Weiss and Parkes distinguish the bereavement experiences of their widows by anticipation of death, they do not further delineate the experience by cause of death. For example, natural deaths which were unanticipated are placed in the same category as accidents. Thus our analysis of bereavement by cause of death is limited to gross categories—suicide versus all other causes by the presence or absence of anticipation of death.

This division between anticipation and non-anticipation of death is possible because for suicide too we find that the act is not always unexpected, and that the degree to which it is expected has important consequences for the widow. Wallace distinguishes between three levels of anticipation or awareness of death—the socially dying (where the relationship had been or was being severed prior to the suicide), the physically dying (where natural death, rather than suicide, was expected to culminate a long illness), and the strangers to death (where neither death nor suicide was expected).

Glick, Weiss, and Parkes report that anticipation is one of the most important determinants of the adequacy of recovery. In cases where death was preceded by illness, death was traumatic but understood [2, p. 258]. It is not so much that anticipation lessens the widow's grief, they argue, but rather the knowledge that death may soon be at hand leads the wife to begin a redefinition of her role. When the inevitable end of the marital relationship could not be ignored, these women were forced to at least imagine a different life.

Secondly, both studies suggest that even if the wife refused to consider the possibility of change, she was nevertheless living a changed life in the period preceding the death because of the hospitalization or nursing of the spouse. Such changes in dependency patterns, in traditional roles, forced them to enter the process and act of decision making. They had to be responsible, and this assumption of responsibility assisted them in their future recovery.

The changed lives of women who must care for their husbands is further evident in Wallace's work on suicide bereavement. Many of the men who suicided were silent partners in marriage. With physical and emotional problems of their own, they offered little help to their wives, yet they demanded a great deal of caring from them. In noting the effects of giving care, Wallace tells us that giving care required long dormant or quite new abilities from the widows. All these women were forced to cope—whether it lay in balancing the checkbook or taking full responsibility for the rearing of their children—and in coping while their husband was still alive, they were better able to manage after he was dead.

But anticipation is a double edged sword. It may help the woman to better manage some aspects of her life, but it may also act against her full "social" recovery. The changes in role which come from anticipation of death and care giving are not without problems. As with those suicide widows who had constructed relationships on their need to care and their husband's need for care, we find that illness redefined relationships in terms of care, too. Glick and his associates also report that women devoted less and less time to other interests and relationships as the husband became their constant preoccupation [2, p. 37]. Prior knowledge of death then is a hindrance to the extent that the woman isolates herself from others whom she will need later as interactive partners. In cutting away from her friends and devoting herself to her husband, she denied herself an important source for recovery. Both studies support this observation.

The relief which may follow death is not often noted in the bereavement literature. For many of the widows of suicide, the death culminated a series of life crises and many were therefore relieved to see the cause of their trauma removed. The relief which also ended their spouse's suffering is evident in the following remarks of one of the suicide widows:

> You tell yourself then, you know they were sick and with something they wouldn't be able to live with. So they suffer, they finish suffering

you know, suffering no more. I believe that it's the same way with people like my husband that finally took his own life; he couldn't bear it no more . . . He couldn't bear the time and the way he was.

A sense of relief is also reported among women who have been bereaved from other kinds of death. Glick states that with debilitating illness the husband's condition had become intolerable for them as well as for him. They then began to wish, even to pray that death would release their husbands from suffering and themselves from the continued witnessing of suffering. This is particularly the case when husbands have had a history of alcoholism. The two widows of alcoholic husbands, in Glick's sample, expressed bitterness over their husband's self destruction, but also said that their deaths had brought relief.

The problem for women in such cases is that *relief is not often accepted as an appropriate bereavement reaction.* "I felt relief, a horrible thing to say" [1, p. 101]. Those who experienced relief reported that it was necessary to mask it. While there may not be great tolerance exhibited towards those who are bereaved, this does not imply that those who show no remorse will be more acceptable.

Unanticipated Deaths

Unanticipated death occasions the most severe bereavement reactions. Glick reports that in these cases, "widows dwelled obsessively on what had happened and continually searched for its cause; widows were unsure it was their husband who had died and it was difficult for them to accept the reality even upon the viewing of the body [2, p. 43]." A sense of the husband's continued presence was a prominent feature of unanticipated deaths. Nine widows in Glick's sample reported feeling that their husbands were alive or near them; all these were cases of unforewarned bereavement. The authors speculate that this lack of opportunity to prepare for loss predisposed these women to the development of a fantasy relationship.

Denial of death is a prominent feature as well among the suicide widows who were strangers to death. Not anticipating widowhood, these women, when catapulted into that status, tried not to think about the death—they denied it. Suicide widows however also had to deny the cause of death, both cause and event creating problems in the reactions of others as well as in themselves. Anger had to be "directed outwardly, against doctors and the police, the medical examiners and the undertakers, against anyone other than the man death robbed them of [1, p. 181]."

In contrast to cases of anticipated death where women were forced to cope, learning in that process that they could manage, those widowed by sudden death were ill prepared for the future they would have to make. Glick notes: "These women especially begin to fear that they could not manage loss and isolation. They fear nervous breakdown. Their trust that the world they live in is predictable and benign has been attacked [2, p. 47] ." With no anticipation of death there had been no role preparation for independence. Thus the grief these women experienced was compounded by their lack of preparation for the future.

Those who were widowed by sudden death had to make sense of a world which had suddenly lost its meaning. However, those who were widowed by suicide were faced with an additional problem—they were forced to make sense of a self-inflicted act. Their ability to invoke closure was further hindered when there was evidence that the deaths might not have been suicides after all. In all three of the cases of strangers to death, the evidence of suicide was problematic but this did not keep the harshness of unanticipated death from being compounded by stigma.

Personal Reactions

Glick found that the immediate reactions of those widowed by natural death or accidents were shock, physical distress, bewilderment and deep despair. While these symptoms were most intense in the days following the death they were later replaced by an all encompassing sorrow.

We find here, and also with suicide, that *emotional distress is accentuated when the woman felt blameworthy*. While all deaths may be said to provoke a review of the prior relationship, the obsessional nature of this review varies with one's sense of responsibility for the death. That feelings of responsibility are not isolated occurrences can be seen in the Glick report that 47 per cent of the widows in his sample gave indications of self reproach. Even eight weeks after their husband's death, they found acts of omission or commission which might have contributed to the death.

But while one may wonder whether forcing her husband to go to the doctor earlier or keeping him from driving an unsafe car might have prevented his death, it is a widely held belief that illness and accidents are events beyond human control and therefore beyond anyone's responsibility. In accidental or natural death hardly anyone will hold the widow responsible. If and when she blames herself, others will remind her that it was not her fault or that it was God's will. By contrast, when suicide has been the cause of death, responsibility becomes a primary issue. In addition it is also difficult *not* to see the death as an attack upon one's self as well as on the past relationship.

In cases of suicide a sense of co-partnership in the death is especially apparent. Those who had left their husbands prior to the suicide wondered if that had precipitated the act; those who were unprepared for death or suicide were left to wonder what they might have contributed towards the act. When we compare the search for explanations by those widowed from suicide versus other forms of death, *the search by widows of suicide is more intense, more solitary and less amenable to resolution than such processes in bereavement in natural or accidental death.*

An indication of the differential intensity of bereavement by suicide may be seen in the occurrence of suicide attempts in these samples. For some of Glick's widows there was a "flirtation with self destruction," but he assures us that there were no suicide attempts and that the widows did not appear to seriously consider it. This is in contrast to Wallace's research where one widow attempted and three widows contemplated suicide. While we cannot conclude from these preliminary studies that a death by suicide is always more likely to occasion self destructive acts by survivors, these data do suggest the more serious effects on survivors of a death by suicide.

Grief is not a constant component in the bereavement experience in either of the two studies. Like loneliness or depression, it is something that descends upon the individual, having been prompted by particular events. Once the period of intense grief passes, a feeling of personal disorganization is common to the widows. One coping tactic that was employed in an effort to minimize such feelings was that of keeping busy. But keeping busy, when it involves interaction with others, presents special problems to those who are bereaved by suicide.

When a death from natural or accidental causes has occurred, one does not usually risk a great deal when she tells another that she is a widow. One may decide not to disclose the fact for fear that the mention of death will make the other uncomfortable, but nevertheless such widows know that disclosure will not result in personal shame. Questions as to cause of death can be answered without fear of self incrimination. There are risks, however, in disclosure for widows of suicide.

> Have I got any pains of stigma? No I think they've accepted it . . . the whole situation. Right from the beginning I think these people, the ones that I did tell it to, have accepted it and they've accepted me so I don't feel this. But . . . as I've said before there were still a couple who I never would tell. Never speak of it, for those reasons [1, p. 210].

Widows of suicide are discreditable. Disclosure poses risks to future encounters. One can never be too sure what the other's reaction may be. It may consist of a repugnance toward the act or it may consist of a battery of probing questions. In any event easy interaction cannot be taken for granted when the problem of disclosure poses such difficulties. The dilemma for the bereaved from suicide is that, although they are in need of others with whom they may share their experiences, they feel such sharing may constitute barriers to interaction and to communication. Either way they resolve their problem, whether by talking or maintaining silence, they risk unhealthy crisis resolutions.

Reactions of Others

Bereavement is a lonely and isolating experience regardless of cause of death. Glick reports that in the first weeks after death other mourners provide support. This initial period of support, however, is brief, as the husband's friends disengage and mutual friends return to their families. Despite the fact that support diminished after the official mourning period had ended, Glick found that the widows in his sample could count on their families for support. In spite of such support, Glick notes that while no widow was totally isolated and although all could count on some source of support, they all had to deal with relational change.

Now being alone, their interaction with others changed. Thus some widows found that their mothers relegated them to their childhood status and attempted to direct their lives. After the death of her husband, a widow often found herself in a battle to maintain her authority vis-a-vis her parents, her in-laws or her children. The relations most changed by widowhood were those with friends. The impact of being single in a coupled society struck these women with particular intensity. Married friends who had been friends of the "couple" were lost; friends who were retained were those the woman had known apart from the context of her marriage. As Glick describes it, the widows recognized that they were no longer as valuable as friends, that their situation in life had changed and with it their capacity to engage in favorable exchanges and to reciprocate sociability. Their concerns were now different, too. In effect, the loss of her husband's relationship is only one of several the woman must sustain as the death of her husband triggers losses in other relational spheres as well.

But while the widows of natural death and accidents faced problems in terms of finding support, the problems faced by the widows of suicide were more severe. Of the suicide widows we find that four of the twelve had no family and that two of these had no close friends either. Three of the twelve were forced to survive without help from family or friends. Of the other nine, eight had two or more friends or family members with whom to talk and the ninth had one. There is little mention in their interviews of family support being available and only some mention of the availability of support from friends. While devoting themselves to the care of their husbands, many of these women had eschewed outside help and had not formed very many friendships of their own. Thus the bereavement experience of these widows followed the same lonely patterns that had been established in their lives prior to the suicide of their husbands.

When friends were available they did provide sources of aid and comfort. But in contrast to the cases of natural death and accidents where explanations for the death were apparent, friends of the suicide widows sometimes insisted upon working out explanations and rationales for the suicide. Their need for an explanation often collided with the widow's needs. Finally there were those who insisted that the widow not talk about the event. In cases such as these, the widow found herself befriended but with little comfort resulting from the friendship.

From both these studies we learn that *there are few good listeners available to bereaved persons.* It is striking that members of the clergy rarely are cited as sources of help. Glick tells us that the clergy seemed to enter only as their ceremonial role required. Wallace does not cite even one instance of a clergy member helping or comforting a widow.

This lack of support for widows may be understandable in cases of suicide where religious prohibitions against the act may make both the widow and the clergyman uncomfortable in each other's presence. But there is no easy explanation for the apparent lack of help in ministering to the needs of those bereaved by other types of death. The obvious conclusion seems to be that those who have closest contact with death—clergymen as well as physicians— are least equipped to deal with it.

An interesting difference between the samples is that the widows in Glick's study cite the funeral director as a source of help. This finding is in direct contrast with the literature which portrays him as a conniver profiting from the sorrows of others. Glick found that nearly all the widows were grateful to the funeral directors for the helpfulness and kindness they displayed. Planning the funeral also helped the woman in the attainment of her self confidence. If the funeral went well and others complimented her on it, she could take heart in the good job that she had done and could focus upon this as evidence of her ability to cope and to recover.

These fine relations with funeral directors stand in direct opposition to Wallace's findings. Except for one woman, the suicide widows did not report their funeral directors to have been helpful and several complained that they had been exploited in their moment of grief. Once again the difference which the cause of death makes is apparent. Having handled the body and seen the death certificate, the funeral director can easily ruin any attempt the widow is making to conceal the cause of death. He is in possession of discrediting information and it is understandable that the widow may feel uncomfortable in his presence. Mutual knowledge of such information—especially since discretion if not concealment is important to one but not to the other—can undermine the basis for any comfortable relationship.

Parallel problems are evident when the suicide widow reported her experiences in dealing with the other death-related officials. One said that the police felt justified in illegally collecting evidence to solve the crime of suicide in her own home before she got there. A second said the medical examiner was particularly callous in reaching his decision that death had been caused by suicide. Officials who decide on death benefits were also reported to have been difficult for these widows to deal with. Even those who brought the news of the death to the widow, no doubt in part because they did not "know what to say", were not seen as helpful by the suicide widow. Whether such "injuries" were real or imagined by the suicide widow makes no difference as in either case the consequent isolation was the same.

Adjustment and Re-involvement

In comparing the adjustment process, the similarity between the samples is less because the time interval studied in the two projects differs. The recovery process delineated by Glick and his associates is based upon follow-up interviews which occurred from two to four years after the husband's death. The recuperative processes which Wallace reported are limited to what occurred after thirteen months of bereavement. Differences or similarities in the adjustment processes exhibited by the widows in these samples may therefore be more a result of differences in time elapsed than they are a result of differences due to cause or anticipation of death. Thus, while a comparison of recovery patterns is worthwhile, considerable caution must be exercised in generalizing from it.

Glick found that, by the end of the first year, most of the widows had returned to fairly active social participation. After conducting follow-up interviews with forty-three of the forty-nine women in their sample they specified several different recovery movement patterns, including movement toward and away from remarriage, reorganization on an intimate non-marital relationship or on a close relationship with one or more kin, reorganization without close relationships, and finally those whose lives at the time of the follow-up interview were chaotic.

Fourteen had already married at the time of the follow-up interview and five more were seen to be headed in that direction although they were not yet engaged. Glick reports that those who remarried had expressed interest in remarriage by the end of the first year of bereavement and had begun dating at about that same time.

Among those who treated widowhood as a permanent status, seventeen had organized their lives "relatively" independent of close relationships with other adults. It is interesting that in assessing the motives of widows who adopted this pattern, the authors do so within the context of whether their widows' reasons for not contemplating marriage are "plausible". The implication throughout their discussion of the movement away from remarriage is that while these patterns may lead toward adequate recovery, they are not as desirable as recovery involving remarriage. Rationales are never asked of the women who wanted to remarry but the women who did not were seen as needing not just an explanation, but a "plausible" one at that.

Glick tells us that five of the widows had reorganized their lives around relationships with kin, but this category is sketchy and we are unsure of whether this attention to relatives implies a reorganization or intensification of previously existing relationships. For example, the authors note the case of Mrs. T. who had been very close to her mother and two sisters prior to her husband's death. That this closeness continued is not surprising and it emphasizes the need to identify patterned change more closely.

In this category, too, the authors' tendency to view remarriage as the least problematic of recoveries is apparent. We are warned that a widow who organizes her life around her mother risks being left alone, usually in her middle age and presumably, from the authors' perspective, when she is a less attractive candidate for remarriage. That second husbands die and that middle aged men can contract fatal illnesses are risks of remarriage which the authors do not consider. A possible reason for their failure to note the risks a widow faces in a second marriage may be their assumption that remarriage is "natural" and that the company of a man is worth the risk of loneliness or hurt which would follow from his death.

Chaotic was the term used to categorize the lives of six widows. The authors note that only one of the women in this group had anticipated the death of her husband, therefore implying the importance of anticipation for recovery. However, they also note that two of the women who did not anticipate their husband's deaths had previous histories of mental instability. Thus we cannot be sure whether previous instability or lack of anticipation of death was the primary determinant in affecting the chaotic condition. Again, the need for more careful delineation of patterns of change is evident.

Despite the above mentioned limitations, Glick tells us that anticipation of death is one of the most important determinants of adequacy of recovery. But again, the sexist bias in the definition of recovery is apparent. "The one critical difference among widows was that those who did not anticipate their husband's death did not move toward remarriage". Continuing, they note that these women "rejected the idea of remarriage even when pressed to remarry by a boyfriend, by their children or by their immediate kin, *even in two cases when they had a child with their boyfriend*" (emphasis not in original).

As we earlier noted, anticipation is an important element in recovery. Thus the authors' explanation that those who have been confounded by an un-expected death are probably less willing to place themselves in a situation where a similar loss might occur is plausible. The difficulty lies in the use of remarriage as the criterion of recovery. If widowed women live adequate lives—by their own accounts—and prefer the maintenance of their status why should any question of remarriage arise? In focusing so closely upon remarriage, the authors reveal more about their own domain assumptions than they do about the determinants of successful adjustment to bereavement.

In turning our attention to the *recovery patterns of suicide widows,* we find that their recovery (again using remarriage as a criterion for comparison purposes) *even when death is anticipated or the relationship has been attenuated is not as likely to be complete or to take place as quickly.* In the suicide cases we find that while *anticipation of death has an impact on the widow's willingness to date, it has little impact upon her professed willingness to marry.*

The seven widows whose husbands were socially dying were quickest to re-engage themselves in social activities. Life began again for them between two and six months after their husband's suicide as they began to make decisions about their lives and what to do with their husband's belongings.

Probably because these widows had disengaged themselves emotionally from their husbands prior to their suicide the widow's life was "on the upswing" thirteen months later. As evidence of their social participation, four of the seven had formed sexually intimate relations with a male and the three others had begun dating. Yet at the end of their first year of bereavement none of these widows were willing to consider remarriage. They had been hurt by their marriages and by their husband's deaths and did not want to be in a situation where a similar hurt might occur. However, even without remarriage these women are portrayed as being on the road to a healthful recovery.

In the two cases where death was anticipated but not suicide—where there was some anticipation that the relationship might soon be ended—the road to recovery was reported by Wallace to be more difficult. One of these widows had an incapacitated daughter who needed considerable care. Her husband's suicide did not affect her functioning because she could not allow it to do so. But while she functioned, Wallace tells us that she could hardly be considered recovered as she had never been able to grieve in the first place. In the other case, while the widow did return to the world of the living, it took her ten months to do so and her search for an understanding of her husband's suicide was marked by anger and bitterness.

Wallace's "strangers to death" are comparable to those widows in Glick's sample who did not anticipate the deaths of their spouses. We find that the bereavement experiences of both types of widows are harsh. Of all the widows of suicide, these widows had the most severe reactions. The severity of their reactions influenced the adjustment process. The three women who fell into this category continued to deny the suicide throughout the year with one at times denying the death itself. Reinvolvement in social activities came most slowly for them. At the close of their first year of bereavement one widow was involved with a man while two insisted that they would never consider remarriage.

Though the authors in either study do not deal with it directly, it seems that many of the problems faced by the widows were related to their status as women and, more particularly, to the way in which traditional sex role behavior is defined. In both studies we hear comments from widows who have begun to go out on their own and have found the experience distasteful. That the reason for their displeasure is related to a view which perceives women as sexual objects should be apparent in the following remarks:

> I think they know you're a widow and a lot of them might want to take you out just for sex. They feel, well, "Gee, I've got a lonely widow and . . . maybe I can help her or something"! And that's all that is on their minds. A couple of fellows I've been introduced to have said, "You're a widow, so you go to bed [2, p. 224]."

> . . . I don't know why it aggravates me, and it shouldn't, but I don't know why men think that if you're not married now that you have to be hard up for sex [1, p. 123].

It is acceptable for a man to enter a bar and strike up conversation or to become a regular at a neighborhood place. Bars and other specified social gathering places are not so easily entered by women. Few enter these places on their own, and, when they do, they are likely to be seen as being on the prowl. Evidence of this phenomenon can be seen in the remarks of one of the suicide widows who bemoaned "the fact that a woman cannot go into any bar in Boston without being considered a pickup by the men there" [1, p. 124]. Even if women do not frequent places which might be thought of as potential pick-up spots, their new single status, as we have seen in the previously quoted remarks, leads to the same designation.

A woman without a male in our society is often seen as unusual and this stigmatization does not escape widows.

> Being a widow is just something extraordinary. You don't belong. You're a widow, you know, as if you were a freak or something . . . I wear my wedding ring all the time. I don't tell people I'm a widow . . . [2, p. 220].

Social life occurs with other couples and the definition of couple is always half male. Given the self hate common in many minority groups, many women do not see other women as friends and this also leads to the widow's isolation. Finally, married women often hold these same conceptions of single women, seeing them as incomplete and/or as a threat. When widows find they are no longer welcome or comfortable among married friends and begin befriending other widows, they are well aware that their status has changed and that other widows are not as valuable as social partners as a male would be.

The solution to these problems faced by the widow is evident from the data presented by these two studies although neither makes this observation. *Recovery is facilitated by both imagined as well as real life independence, in identity, role, and relationship.* Whether the woman is caring for her husband, working at a job, being mother to her children, or relating to her family or close friends, such acts provide the necessary context for recovery. In other words, *for women to be prepared for widowhood, they must live more complete lives as people,* rather than having their identity defined as partner to a pair.

Future Bereavement Research

While these two studies have yielded some valuable observations into the problems of bereavement by suicide and other forms of death, their generalizability is limited by some methodological problems.

First their samples suffer the failing that afflicts so much sociological research in that they are drawn primarily from the lower and middle classes.

Glick states that "when the occupational distribution of those in the sample is compared with the occupational distribution of the Boston area population we find the sample to be somewhat fuller in blue collar occupations".

The suicide widows too are not representative of the class hierarchy. Limiting ourselves to employment as an indicator, we find the job distribution of these women ranges from factory worker to teacher. The jobs of their husbands reflect a similar range from laborer to middle level white collar positions.

Of course, it may be that the attainment of a wide distribution of suicide cases is an impossibility. As Wallace and others have noted, definitions of phenomenon such as suicide cannot be taken for granted. The components necessary for certification of death by suicide are not clear and designations may be determined by contingencies far removed from the actual means employed to induce death.

It remains true that sociologists, after all, have never been terribly success-ful in interviewing those of higher social status and class positions. Especially in the classification of death by suicide, where power, class and status are important determinants we must be weary of generalizing our findings to too large a universe as an important sector has been neglected in the already assembled research.

Sociology, in many respects, has been a science limited to the study of whomever is available. In studying bereavement we must recognize that we are operating under similar constraints. Describing the class distribution of their sample, Glick theorizes that "it may be that early death is disproportionately a blue collar experience". While this may have some credence, and while it may explain the disproportionate number of working class widows in their sample, it is likely that, even if this were not the case, we would still have a sociology of bereavement which centers upon the lower end of the spectrum as members of the upper class are rarely available or amenable to being interviewed.

There are other problems, in addition to that of representativeness, in these studies. Death and dying occur as do so many phenomena of social life, within social networks. One cannot rely solely upon the perception of one member for a full account of a social relationship. A member's perception is limited by his/her own interpretations and, as the sociology of knowledge reminds us, these interpretations are influenced by many factors. To elucidate definitions of the situation, we must be familiar with the environmental conditions in which the definition took place. By focusing upon past hoc accounts we obtain only a partial account of these conditions.

Obviously, in studying bereavement, we are limited in that the dead person cannot be contacted for his account of what has occurred. However, his views could be elicited before the death has occurred. If one wants to understand bereavement a project might begin before the loss has occurred, for example, in the terminal ward of a hospital, and then proceed to interview the family in the following months. In cases where suicide is expected or attempts have been made, these families might be contacted so that the processual nature of family life might be tapped.

This emphasis upon the family is not accidental. What is needed in the area of bereavement research is the approach Jules Henry used so effectively in his depiction of autistic children—an immersion into the lives of the bereaved in their home territories both before the event and certainly after it has occurred—in order to delineate the factors contributing to particular modes of adjustment.

The efficacy of the network approach and the need for its inclusion in research of this kind can be seen, for example, in the ways in which the impact of children on bereavement is broached in the studies under consideration.

Both studies allude to the presence of children. Glick found that children often make successful bereavement less likely, but that the widows he interviewed believed their presence was an impetus for recovery. Little attention is paid in either study to the effect that loss has on children or to the effect that their perception of the situation has on the mother's subsequent adjustment. In *After Suicide* we learn from the widows that the men who suicided were often unkind to their children. We never learn the children's perception of the situation.

We must remember that adjustment to bereavement does not occur in isolation and that accounts themselves are precipitated by interactive situations where actors feel called upon to explain or justify some aspects of their behavior. Of course, interviewing many or all members within the family network will not give us the "truth" about the preceding relationship or the subsequent bereavement patterns—at best we will only have more accounts which are all situationally determined—but the gathering of accounts of all the interested parties may give us greater insight as to the reasons for the emergence of particular accounts. Clearly with respect to sociological research in bereavement, much work remains to be done.

REFERENCES

1. S. E. Wallace, *After Suicide,* Wiley-Interscience, New York, 1973.
2. I. O. Glick, R. S. Weiss and C. M. Parkes, *The First Year of Bereavement,* Wiley-Interscience, New York, 1974.

CHAPTER 9

Social Organization
and Death[1]

Vanderlyn R. Pine

The imminence and occurrence of death give rise to a wide variety of beliefs and practices. These differences are most apparent as they exist in different societies. For, as Durkheim (1951) long ago pointed out, different social organizations engender different reactions to death-related phenomena. It is the intention of this paper to examine and discuss the ways in which important variations in social organization and demography of societies are related to the beliefs and practices of their members toward dying and death.

It is important in addressing this issue to clearly delineate what we understand as "social organization." Social organization has (at least) three levels. First, there is the individual or interpersonal level which largely involves everyday interactions and the usual face-to-face roles one plays. Second, there is the group level, which is, of course, dependent on the individual level, but which involves relationships among and between groups of individuals. Third, there is the societal or social order level, which involves general patterns of group existence as characterized by the organization of an entire community or society. One of the major contentions of this paper is that beliefs and practices of the members of a society toward dying and death are largely dependent upon the society's social organization.

Hertz (1960) points out that among tribes that are largely organized around physical agricultural activities, very old people not only are mourned differently once they have died, but also that when they are in the process of dying they are largely excluded from social activities. Thus, when their death does occur, it is considerably less disruptive to the overall society.

Glaser and Strauss (1965) point out that in American society, which is largely organized around institutions other than the family, e.g., hospitals, etc., the treatment of dying patients is largely institutionalized, and they are to a great extent eliminated from active society. Sudnow (1967, 72-77) emphasizes this point in his discussion of "social death," which occurs when the "social organization of dying" effectively isolates a biologically living human organism to the extent that it may be considered "dead and gone" by the members of its social groups and by society at large.

Demographic considerations of such vital statistics as the birth rate and the death rate also have certain important implications for beliefs and practices involving dying and death. Weber (1947, 93-4) comments that "human mortality . . . is naturally of the very greatest sociological importance through the various ways in which human action has been oriented to these facts." Hertz (1960), Malinowski (1948), and Firth (1964) all emphasize that in societies in which death occurs to relatively young individuals who are still important to the workings of society, their loss is considered an important one and "shakes the solidarity" of the group to the point that the beliefs and practices surrounding death are largely aimed at reintegrating the group's sense of cohesiveness.

The social and cultural values of various societies are important in determining the manner in which people of that society conduct themselves at the time of death. Obligatory social rituals at the time of death seem to represent tributes to the life value or human "net worth" of the living as well as the dead. In addition, they also serve as severance rites to separate the dead from the living. As such, these funeral rituals become a rite of passage, and they are intended to assist mourners through their bereavement (see VanGennep, 1960).

Social observers have long recognized the functions of funeral rites and practices (Durkheim, 1961; Firth, 1964; Malinowski, 1948), and while funerals are created by death, they are regulated by social factors. This is because the problems of death are not solely individual, but have social consequences as well. Malinowski (1948, 53) explains:

> [Death] . . . threatens the very cohesion and solidarity of the group . . . [and the funeral] counteracts the centrifugal forces of fear, dismay, demoralization, and provides the most powerful means of reintegration of the group's shaken solidarity and of reestablishment.

Malinowski (1948) points out that the kinship organization of society is an important factor in determining that society's rules of incest, and that incest violations are so serious a disruptive element to the social organization of most primitive societies, that although suicide is not an everyday activity, the discovery of an incest violation often eliminates the inhibition to commit suicide and results in just that. Thus, the power of the group over the individual regarding dying is importantly connected to the social organization of that society.

It is in the funeral that death reactions become visible in most societies.[2] Funeral rites allow the bereaved to pass through the period of adjustment following death with a defined social role, delimit the period of mourning, allow the bereaved to release grief emotions publicly, and aim at helping to commemorate an individual's passing. Funeral rites also provide an occasion for group assembly, reaffirm social values, and allow for relief from the guilt that is often a part of bereavement. As Firth (1964, 63) explains, "a funeral rite is a social rite *par excellence*. Its obstensible object is the dead person, but it benefits not the dead but the living."

Firth (1964, 63-64) goes on to describe some of the important aspects of the funeral. First, there is "the resolution of uncertainties in the behavior of the immediate kin, by providing social support in the form of funeral ritual." Second, there is "the fulfillment of social sequence . . . by stressing the dead, they emphasize the value of the services of the living." And third, there is "the social importance of the economic aspect . . . [which] is not incidental . . . [for] every funeral means expenditure." (For fuller discussions see Sjoberg, 1960, 262-3; Pine, 1969; and Pine and Phillips, 1970.)

In spite of the cultural differences, the following generalized schema is applicable to a number of cultures and societies (for a fuller discussion see Pine, 1969). Death gives rise to personal emotional responses, which initiate culturally oriented responses and reactions, which evolve into specific mortuary patterns. Every culture has tradional customs for handling death, and as grief ensues, societally based reactions tend to be demonstrated in the form of funeral practices. These customary practices aim at providing structures upon which bereaved persons may lean, hopefully providing a sense of consolation and easing the transition caused by the termination of personal interaction.

Blauner (1966, 378) observes: "Since mortality tends to disrupt the ongoing life of social groups and relationships, all societies must develop some forms of containing its impact." He then goes on to point out that "mortuary institutions are addressed to the specific problems of the disposal of the dead *and* the rituals of transition from life to death." Funeral rites, then, attempt to give support not merely to the next-of-kin, but to the community as well.

Hertz (1960) describes the practice of provisional burial and emphasizes the fact that this practice and other attitudes toward death are influenced largely by the social organization. One of the interesting organizational features of these societies is that the deceased is actually part of the living organization of society, since he influences people's behavior until the final burial. This situation is the exact reverse of the one described by Sudnow (1967, 72-77) involving social death. On the one hand, biological death precedes the termination of social (organizational) interaction, while on the other, biological death follows social death.

This emphasizes the importance of the way in which the society is organized. That is, among the provisional burial tribes, death occurs primarily to the young, and the demographic pattern is such that the loss of an individual is an important loss to society as a whole. This gives rise to beliefs and practices which continue to include the deceased in social activities. Among societies where death occurs primarily to those who are an important part of the community social organization, i.e., the young, there is an unwillingness to release the dead from their obligations to society. On the other hand, in a society where death comes primarily to people who have lost their value to the community organization, i.e., the old, there is a tendency to exclude the living but inert (socially dead) human organism. It appears, therefore, that it is not so much the value of life that is at question, but rather the importance that individuals have for a given social organization.

Another organizational characteristic which influences beliefs and practices surrounding dying and death is the extent to which the society is formally organized. Specifically, in societies that are organized around bureaucratic structures and highly formal institutions, the impact of the death of an individual is considerably diminished no matter how much his loss might mean to the other individuals with whom he interacts on an interpersonal level.

This is the case in the United States where the handling of illness and death are increasingly the responsibility of institutions other than the family (see Glaser and Strauss, 1965; Fulton, 1965; and Sudnow, 1967). At the same time, and partially as a result of the same social forces, death comes primarily to the old. The general elimination of infant and child mortality and greater control over the diseases of adolescence and middle life, work to concentrate death in the ranks of the elderly. There is also a general absence of *direct* contact in American life with death resulting from war.

In this regard, Parsons points out that there are a number of problems arising because of the structural nature of American social organization. He (1963, 61) points to the fact that this is largely due to the demographic facts that exist because of the "demographic revolution" of the past century, "characterized by passage from a high-birth-rate, high-death-rate balance to one of vastly lower death rates, and where something of a balance is maintained, necessarily much lower birth rates."

What this means, of course, is that Americans must face death much less often than previously. As with any experience, less contact with something means less familiarity with how to cope with it. Parsons (1963) points out that one of the important reasons for this change is the advancement of medical science. Moreover, the institutionalized structural arrangement of American culture has changed to the point that science (and medicine) are elavated to a very high level. In this sense, then, the demographic changes which are largely the result of technological advancements, are accompanied by vast social organizational changes in the arrangement and configuration of institutions which influence behavior.

Another demographic change is important. Namely, many of the recent changes have contributed to the fact that an increasingly large proportion of the population is located in the "retired" category. There have been vast structural changes to that section of the population *no longer* employed in the active work force. At present, these people are not a part of the "dynamic" sector of the social organization, but are alive and relatively healthy instead of having the former "one foot in the grave" (for a more detailed discussion see Parsons, 1963; and Blauner, 1963). The presence in society of such individuals cannot help but modify the attendant beliefs and practices toward dying and death. Specifically, there appears to be more "denial" of death among these people (Fulton, 1965, 89-111).

In addition to the diminished presence of dying and death in America, Fulton (1965) and Sudnow (1967) point out that there is an increasing utilization of "death" experts, i.e., funeral directors. Thus, there is an occupational specialist whose position in the table of social organization is to be an impersonal emissary to death, thereby reducing what "must be done." Furthermore, Gorer (1965) argues that the changes in the social structure have fostered changes in the ceremonial observances surrounding the dead. Pine and Phillips (1970) explain that mourning dress is rare; there is less formal cancellation of social engagements for a predetermined period; and visits to the house of mourning and the respectful viewing of the body have declined. Furthermore, in our diffuse society, participation in funerals is increasingly restricted to family members and friends rather than involving the larger community. Consequently, family members must shoulder a greater emotional burden than in the past. Funerals are shorter and involve considerably less religious ritual than they once did. Largely because of the decline in a sacred outlook in favor of a secular one, there is a decreasing belief in life after death (Glock and Stark, 1960). Thus, the bereaved cannot comfort themselves with thoughts about an "after-life." In short, ceremonial, religious, and organizational responses to death have lost significance in American society.

However, even though death appears less disruptive to society (Goffman, 1966), it has become more serious for bereaved individuals. For with all of these societal changes, one thing remains the same: Sooner or later, most people will experience death as it removes from them a spouse, parent, child, other relative, or friend. Blauner (1966, 390) explains what this means for the bereaved: "He experiences grief less frequently, but more intensely, since his emotional involvements are not diffused over an entire community, but are usually concentrated on one or a few people."

Pine and Phillips (1970) argue that *because* Americans increasingly lack both the ceremonial and social mechanisms and arrangements that once existed to help them cope with death, such things as monetary expenditures have taken on added importance as a means for allowing the bereaved to express, to others as well as themselves, their sentiments for the deceased. For with limited modes of expression available, the bereaved find it increasingly difficult to provide evidence of their concern for both the dead and the conventional standards of decency in their community. Thus, funeral practices are again seen to be influenced by the social organization of society.

Death is one of the most important social occasions in life, and its occurence provides an occasion for socially conditioned grief reactions and mourning practices. While funerals are created by death, they are *regulated* by social factors, because the problems of death are not solely individual but have broad social consequences as well. The deceased becomes the focal point for the attention of the bereaved. Dying and death, however, involve not only individuals, but also the society of which they are a part. Thus, in addition to individual psychological reactions to dying and death, there are important social forces that affect the beliefs and practices of society members toward dying and death.

NOTES

1. The preparation of this paper was partially facilitated by a National Institutes of Health Fellowship No. 1 F01 MH38124-01A1 from the National Institute of Mental Health.

2. For more complete accounts of religion and funeral customs, see Malinowski, 1948, especially pp. 47-53; Habenstein and Lamers, 1960; Fulton, 1963; and Gorer, 1965.

REFERENCES

Blauner, Robert. Death and social structure. *Psychiatry*, 1966, *29*, 378-394.

Durkheim, Emile. *Suicide*. New York: The Free Press, 1951.

———, *The elementary forms of the religious life*. New York: Collier Books, 1961.

Firth, Raymond. *Elements of social organization*. Boston: Beacon Press, 1964.

Fulton, Robert. *Death and identity*. New York: John Wiley and Sons, 1965.

Glaser, Barney G. and Strauss, Anselm L. *Awareness of dying*. Chicago: Aldine Publishing Co., 1965.

Glock, Charles and Stark, Rodney. Is there an American protestantism? *Transaction*, 1960. *3*, 8-13.

Goffman, Irwin. Suicide motives and categorization of the living and dead in the United States. Unpublished manuscript, 1966.

Gorer, Geoffrey. *Death, grief and mourning*. Garden City, New York: Doubleday and Company, 1965.

Habenstein, Robert W. and Lamers, William M. *Funeral customs the world over*. Milwaukee: Bulfin Printers, Inc., 1960.

Hertz, Robert. *Death and the right hand*. Glencoe: The Free Press, 1960.

Malinowski, Bronislaw. *Magic, science and religion*. Garden City, New York: Doubleday and Co., Inc., 1948.

Mead, Margaret. *Coming of age in Samoa*. New York: New American Library, 1949.

Parsons, Talcott. Death in American society—A brief working paper. *The American Behavioral Scientist*, 1963, *6*, 61-65.

Pine, Vanderlyn R. Comparative funeral practices. *Practical Anthropology*, 1969, *16*, 49-62.

Pine, Vanderlyn R. and Phillips, Derek. The cost of dying: A sociological analysis of funeral expenditure. *Social Problems*, 1970, *17*, 405-417.

Sjoberg, Gideon, *The preindustrial city*. New York: The Free Press, 1960.

Sudnow, David. *Passing on: The social organization of dying*. Englewood Cliffs, New Jersey: Prentice-Hall, 1967.

VanGennep, Arnold. *The rites of passage*. Chicago: University of Chicago Press, 1960.

Weber, Max. *The theory of social and economic organization*. New York: The Free Press, 1947.

CHAPTER 10

The Street Corner:
A Laboratory for
the Study of
Life-Threatening
Behavior[1]

Robert Kastenbaum
and
Laura Briscoe

How much have we actually learned about dying, death, and lethal behavior in the past quarter-century of research effort? This question is difficult to answer because we have relied overmuch upon a limited spectrum of strategy and procedure. Attitudinal studies have been quite popular, along with semi-structured clinical investigations. It is conceivable that we have acquired by these means some useful insights and dependable findings, but it is difficult to sort out facts and arti-facts without the perspective that would be provided by converging lines of research.

Among the types of research that deserve priority attention, we suggest the following:

---

[1] An earlier version of this paper was prepared for the conference on "Death Research: Methods and Substance," Berkeley, California, March 21-23, 1973.

1. *Authentic developmental studies combining longitudinal with appropriate add-on cohorts to improve our understanding of the relationship between individual and contextual dynamics.* Strictly speaking, we appear to have *no* studies of this type. Lester (1971) has compared responses to a death questionnaire given by students at the same college in 1935 and 1970. This is an interesting exercise and perhaps all that one can do without a substantial research support program. But we really seem to know next to nothing about the development of death-relevant attitudes, thoughts, and behaviors throughout the life-span, with appropriate attention to cultural dynamics and secular change.

2. *Experimental as contrasted with descriptive approaches, the actual manipulation of variables.* A few laboratory experiments have been conducted over the years, such as the pioneering efforts of Alexander and his colleagues (1957; 1959), and more recent studies by Paris & Goodstein (1966), and Lester & Lester (1970). Overall, however, astonishingly little has been done that can be described as experimental.

3. *Studies which relate attitudes or thoughts about death to behavior or social action.* Until we have conducted many studies of this type it will be difficult if not impossible to judge whether a particular attitude toward death actually predicts behavior (and vice-versa). At present, it is tempting to interpret attitudinal results as being virtually identical with overt behavior, a highly questionable procedure.

4. *Naturalistic observations of the actual behavior in which we are interested.* In some areas, we do have fairly direct observations of death-relevant phenomena. The "dying situation" has been observed in various ways by Hinton (1970), Glaser & Strauss (1965; 1968), Kubler-Ross (1969), Weisman (1972), Weisman & Kastenbaum (1968), and many others. However, few such observations have been made in the realm of life-threatening behavior per se. We learn about suicides, "accidental" fatalities and other "unscheduled" deaths after they occur; the behaviors themselves are not available for our direct observation.

Purpose of This Study

The small study reported here addresses itself to the last pair of research needs mentioned above: relationship between background predispositions and actual behavior, and the naturalistic observation of death-relevant phenomena. It was a methodological and perhaps quasi-philosophical exercise rather than an attempt to contribute definitive evidence about a particular type of content. Our reasoning can be summarized as follows:

1. Let us see if we can locate a situation in which life-threatening behavior is out in the open—observable to any person who takes the trouble to notice what is happening. Ideally, this should be a situation in which:

    a. All the relevant behavior is visible;
    b. The time-space dimensions are within a reasonable scope;
    c. Numerous instances of the behavior occur;
    d. The behavior itself includes a considerable range of life-threatening vs life-guarding possibilities;
    e. Replication and generalization to other similar situations are relatively easy to manage;
    f. Both the finesse and scope of the study could be extended, depending upon specific research objectives and the resources available;
    g. The situation offers possibilities for experimental manipulations in the future, although these were not intended for the first study;
    h. The study should cost little or nothing, apart from the time and efforts of the researchers.

2. Let us see if we can test one major hypothesis against another, although in a very preliminary way. This should be a hypothesis in the realm of life-threatening behavior.

These concerns led to the identification of a behavioral situation and a fairly specific set of experimental questions. At this point, we will reverse the usual sequence, and describe the research setting first.

The Research Setting

We fastened upon street-crossing behavior as the phenomena to be observed. This type of behavior appears to meet the criteria listed above. It is also one of the most commonly-available behaviors for observation, and a behavior that often enough is interrupted or terminated by contact with a motor vehicle to constitute a reasonable instance of risk-taking or life-threatening behavior.

The physical setting was comprised of the corner of Woodward Avenue and Putnam Street in Detroit, Michigan. Woodward Avenue is a major artery of traffic that runs from downtown Detroit to the suburbs and connects to up-state routes. Putnam Street intersects with Woodward adjacent to the campus of Wayne State University. This large university is flanked by other buildings and institutions that attract both vehicular and pedestrian traffic (The Institute of Arts, Board of Education Building, Historical Museum, etc).

Woodward-at-Putnam thus offered itself as a convenient location to observe street-crossing behavior in a highly trafficked environment—automobiles, trucks, buses, and pedestrians flowing into this area from every possible direction.

The setting included a traffic signal light and crosswalks at the corner. Although the theoretical focus of observation was at the crosswalk, the observer surveyed street-crossing behavior from the intersection down to the eastward (downtown side) of the street.

The observer would stand on the corner, back toward the Board of Education Building, and have from this position a clear enough view of the pedestrian traffic. Ordinarily, automobiles were parked in every available place on both sides of Woodward, and buses would often pull up on both sides of the street to accept and disgorge passengers within a few feet of the intersection.

The Research Problems

Two basic questions were asked:

1. Is there an empirical relationship between street-crossing behavior and personal characteristics that do not yield themselves to direct observation?

2. Does the weight of evidence suggest that life-threatening behavior (as exemplified by degree of risk-taking in crossing the street) is a molar and consistent characteristic of the individual, *or*, rather, a fairly specific behavior pattern elicited by the specific environmental setting?

These questions are somewhat interdependent, of course. Each question can also be analyzed into component problems, e.g., the relationship between a socio-demographic characteristic and the observable behavior, or the relationship between an on-going covert process and the observable behavior. One could also discuss these questions in light of the hoary mind-body problem, or in the even more flickering light of contemporary research on suicide, accidents, and other identifiable forms of lethal behavior. However, we will proceed directly to the further specification of the research method and the results.

Procedure

On the basis of a pilot study, it was found that street-crossing behavior in this environment could be classified reliably into five discrete categories. These were designated simply as Type A, Type B, Type C, Type D, and Type E modes of street crossing. Each mode was defined by a set of observable behaviors, involving, it seemed to us, a minimum of inference.

According to this classification scheme, the Type A mode included no observable life-threatening maneuvers, while Type E demonstrated the most potent combination of life-threatening actions. The other Types were intermediate, as indicated by their designations.

THE TYPE A PEDESTRIAN:

Stood on the curb until the light changed in his favor;

Glanced briefly at the on-coming traffic in the nearest lanes;

Immediately entered the cross-walk;

Moved across at a moderate-to-brisk pace;

Checked out traffic from the opposite-direction lanes before reaching the half-way point;

Exhibited no erratic or dilatory behaviors.

THE TYPE E PEDESTRIAN:

Stepped out from some location other than the corner;

From between parked cars;

With the traffic light against him;

And without looking in either direction.

Observer would classify Pedestrian's behavior as soon as the street-crossing was completed—and then approach Pedestrian for a brief on-the-spot interview. Observer would explain simply that she was a student who was studying behavior on the streets of a city, and would appreciate a few moments of his or her time. The specific questions she asked will be indicated in the results section.

The observational plan was to obtain a sample of 25 pedestrians in each of the five categories, using the daylight hours only.

Results

PARTICIPANTS

The participants in this study were 125 men and women whose street-crossing behavior was observed, and who consented to the brief interview. Perhaps surprisingly, only one person approached for the interview refused, a man who said he was in a big hurry.

The mean age of the participants was 25, with a range from 17 to 55. In this predominately youthful sample, only five participants reported an age of

45 or older. The Type C crossers had a mean age of 29, highest of all the groups, while the lowest age, 21, characterized the Type E crossers. For what it may be worth, the mean age of the D and E crossers, combined, was 22, as compared with a combined mean of 27 for the other three groups. The "best" crossers (Type A), however, were a little younger than the B's and C's.

There were 55 females and 70 males in the overall sample. (As implied in the preceding section, we were sampling configurations of behavior, not age or sex groups.) The most disproportionate representation of the sexes occurred in the extremes. Of the 25 greatest risk-takers, only 7 were women—while 14 were among the safest pedestrians. On the basis of these very limited findings, it would appear that young women tend to take a more life-guarding approach to street-crossing than do young men in an urban environment, although there are, of course, men and women in all the categories.

SELF-RATINGS OF RISK-TAKING BEHAVIOR IN THE STREET-CROSSING SITUATION

All participants were asked two self-rating questions regarding their just-completed traversal of the street: "How aware were you that you were crossing the street *while* you were crossing the street?" "How safe or risky was your crossing?"

Awareness-of-crossing behavior was expressed on a four-point scale. Because there were 25 participants in each of the Types, it is convenient to express the findings here and on other questions in the terms of percentages (4% for each participant in a particular response category).

The self-rating of safety-hazard was expressed on a five-point scale. In each case, a response categorized as "1" indicated a high degree of safety consciousness: "very aware" of crossing, or "I did cross very safely." Results are given in Tables 1 and 2.

Table 1. Level of Awareness that Observed Actually was Crossing Street (in %)

Level	Type A	Type B	Type C	Type D	Type E
1	20	0	0	0	0
2	68	64	40	32	16
3	12	24	36	44	28
4	0	12	24	24	56

The results are quite clear: People who did cross the street relatively safely—according to the Observer's classification—reported themselves as more aware of their actions, and also as safer, more self-protecting. More than half the

Table 2. Self-Rated Safety of Street Crossing

Level	Type A	Type B	Type C	Type D	Type E
1	76	24	8	4	0
2	24	56	32	24	16
3	0	20	56	48	44
4	0	0	4	20	32
5	0	0	0	4	8

Type E crossers, for example, considered themselves barely aware that they were, in fact, crossing the street, and none considered themselves to have made a really safe crossing.

GENERALITY OF LIFE THREATENING BEHAVIOR: SELF-RATINGS

The participants were asked several questions about the degree of risk-taking in which they engage in situations other than the just-observed street crossing. The first of these questions: "The way you cross the street just now—is this pretty much the way you usually cross streets?" Results are given in Table 3.

Table 3. Relationship Between Observed and Typical Street-Crossing Behavior

Self-Report	Type A	Type B	Type C	Type D	Type E
Typical	100	92	60	64	72
Fairly Typical	0	8	12	28	20
Not Typical	0	0	28	8	8

In general, it appears that observation of a single street-crossing episode fairly well represents the pedestrian's characteristic pattern, at least, according to the pedestrian himself. It is difficult not to be struck by the fact that 100% consistency was reported by the Type A crossers. Those who made a crossing riskier than A or B reported themselves as somewhat less consistent (though not with perfect linearity), but the sample as a whole reported a sense of consistency within the individual from one street-crossing to another.

The participants were next asked to rate their safety vs risk-takingness when they were behind the wheel of an automobile. Those who rated themselves as the safest possible kind of driver ranged in percentage from 78% for Type A down to 4% for D and E, after intermediary stops at 41% and 21%. In other words, the safer the pedestrian, the safer the driver. It should be kept in mind that this close relationship involves data from two different spheres: self-rating of driver safety and Observer's objective classification of pedestrian behavior. The range also appears to be remarkable—only 1 of the

25 Type E crossers classified himself as a really safe driver, while this was the typical response of the A's. (The basis for percentages on this question differ slightly from Type to Type because not all, though most, pedestrians also were motorists.)

The participants were then asked a more general question: "How much of the time do you consider your life to be in danger, in jeopardy?" The response was in terms of estimated % of time during a typical week. The lowest mean % of endangered time was reported by Type A pedestrians, the highest by Type E. From A through E the percentages were: 2.1%; 3.0%; 6.6%; 9.0%; 16.1%. This again is a linear progression. It is striking that approximately eight times as much exposure to danger in their total life situation was reported by E as contrasted with A pedestrians.

All three questions in this group had the same directionality. The participants appeared to see quite a bit of consistency between the risk-taking characteristics of the observed situation, and their more general life patterns, and the direction was entirely in keeping with the behavioristic classifications made prior to the interviews.

CHARACTERISTIC MOOD: SELF-RATING

One question was asked in the realm of affect or mood: "As you go through life, how much of the time do you have a sense of frustration? Think about a typical week, for example." Results are given in Table 4. It can be seen that the "safe" pedestrians reported much lower levels of frustration in life than did the risk-taking crossers. None of the people who reported themselves as characteristically very frustrated crossed the street in either the A, B, or C patterns, while only 1 of 50 people in the D/E patterns reported freedom from frustration.

Table 4. Sense of Frustration in Life

Level of Frustration	Type A	Type B	Type C	Type D	Type E
Almost always	0	0	0	16	16
Usually	0	0	12	20	32
Often	4	16	40	32	32
Occasionally	24	40	36	32	16
Seldom	72	44	12	0	4

LIFE-THREATENING BEHAVIORS ACTUALLY EXPERIENCED: SELF-REPORT

The participants were asked two direct questions about types of life-threatening behaviors they may have already experienced in their lives. They were asked first, *"Have you ever attempted or contemplated suicide?"* (This question fails to differentiate between "attempters" and "thinkers," but appeared to be as far as we could go in this particular research situation.)

The results once more formed a pattern that has become familiar from findings already given here: more suicidal thoughts/actions reported by the riskier pedestrians. From Type A through E we find the following percentages of pedestrians who report either thoughts or attempts: 8%; 12%; 16%; 24%; 32%. In other words, four times as many pedestrians who made the E crossing admitted to suicidal orientations as compared with the A's.

The other question in this set was: *"Have you ever been involved in an automobile accident when you were the driver?"* If we distinguish only between accident/no accident, then we find that five of the 25 "safest crossers" reported accidents, and eight of the almost-as-safe Type B pedestrians. There is a marked increase when we turn to the C's and D's, each of which group has 17 members who report self-involved automobile accidents. The E's? All of the 23 E-crossers who operate automobiles reported at least one accident!

But we can also look into the number of accidents reported, in other words, multiple as well as single accidents in the career of a particular driver. The results are equally striking. None of the A pedestrians reported more than a single accident, while 19 of the 23 driving E's reported two or more accidents: a total of 61 automobile accidents (as compared with the A's five.)

SUBJECTIVE LIFE EXPECTANCIES

The pedestrians were asked two questions that are routinely included in the battery of attitudinal measures developed at the Center for Psychological Studies of Dying, Death, and Lethal Behavior at Wayne State University: "To what age do you *expect* to live?" "To what age would you *like* to live?" The means for each form of subjective life expectancy (SLE) are given in Table 5.

Table 5. Subjective Life Expectancies

SLE	Type A	Type B	Type C	Type D	Type E
Expect to live	81	77	72	69	67
Want to live	92	89	82	77	69

The first inspection shows us that the safer pedestrians *expect* to reach a more advanced age than the riskier pedestrians—a fourteen year difference between the extremes. We also see that all groups, on the average, prefer to live longer than they expect to live. There is approximately a decade's difference between expect and want until we come to the E's, who want only two more years than they expect.

But we should also check out the relationship between SLE and the participant's chronological age at the time of the study. In Table 6 we are able to see

Table 6. Subjective Life Expectancies Relative to Chronological Age

SLE	Type A	Type B	Type C	Type D	Type E
Expect to live	56	50	43	44	46
Want to live	67	62	53	54	48

both forms of SLE re-calculated in terms of distance (in time) from chronological age to death.

With this relativistic view of SLE, we see that the essential differences among pedestrian types remains. Whether calculated in absolute terms, or expressed relative to chronological age, the safe pedestrians both expect and want to live longer than those who take greater risks.

MARITAL STATUS

Finally, we take one indice from the socio-demographic realm: marital status. In Table 7 we see marital status by pedestrian type.

Table 7. Marital Status

Marital Status	Type A	Type B	Type C	Type D	Type E
Married	14	11	8	6	3
Single	10	8	9	16	19
Divorced	1	2	4	1	1
Separated	0	2	3	2	1
Widowed	0	2	1	0	1

It is evident that the safer pedestrians are "more married" and "less single" than the risk-takers. Thus, differences related to the objective classification of life-threatening behavior in one research center can predict marital status as well as life history and phenomenological states. If we see a person engaged in a Type E crossing, we can lay three-to-one adds that this person is single. (At least, if we are standing on the corner of Woodward and Putnam in Detroit.)

Discussion

We will limit discussion to a few main points.

1. This study seems to demonstrate the feasibility of using public space as a natural laboratory for the observation of life-threatening behavior. The particular setting we selected is one that is easily available to other observers (both the Woodward/Putnam corner, and other street corners around the world). By no means, however, do we intend to imply that street-crossing behavior is the

only type of relevant behavior that can be studied naturalistically and system-atically; it is merely our illustrative case.

2. More preliminary and peripheral research was carried out than reported here, especially on the socio-physical characteristics of the environment. There is much room for refinement and also for experimental intervention in "natural laboratories" such as the one illustrated here. Future studies should not be reined in by the limited scope of the research that has been sketched in this chapter.

3. The results, taken within the general limitations of the study, lend strong support to the proposition that observable behavior *is* related to psychosocial characteristics that are less amenable to direct observation. This seems to hold true in all the realms sampled here: marital status, concurrent phenomenologi-cal state, characteristic psychological state, and life history incidents.

4. The relationships between directly observed behavior and the other variables are non-commutable: prediction does not work as well in both directions as it does in one direction. We will not go into the detail that would be required for a thorough exploration of this problem. To return to a previ-ous example, however, we saw that marital status could be predicted (post-dicted, actually) very well from observed street-crossing behavior: the reverse direction of prediction is less adequate. In systematic studies of the kind illus-trated here, one should carefully deal with the direction of prediction and its implications. However, it is worth acknowledging that, in a limited but relative-ly clear way, we have been able to demonstrate a set of consistent relation-ships between predispositions and what people actually do. Seeing how a person crosses the street, we can make a number of "good guesses" about his marital status, mental contents, driving habits, suicidal history, etc. Knowing his mental contents, level of frustration, or driving habits, we can make a good guess as to how he will cross the street.

5. We were impressed by the willingness of pedestrians not only to give their time to the interview but also to express a number of not entirely flatter-ing things about themselves. Whatever else might be said about the high risk-taker, for example, he cannot be characterized as self-deluded. The typical "risky crosser" saw himself as a person whose life is often in jeopardy, and who contributes to this jeopardy himself.

6. The relationship between type of crossing and SLE is richly deserving of further empirical and theoretical analysis. It is one of the areas of this study that touches most closely upon the question of intentionality (Shneidman, 1963). Although we have published two studies that give explicit attention to SLE (Teahan & Kastenbaum, 1971; Sabatini & Kastenbaum, 1973), we have not yet started to do justice to the problem.

7. The weight of converging evidence in this study suggests that life-threatening behavior is not simply called forth by a particular environmental setting. Rather, there is a patterned characteristic of the individual that has an

important bearing on the probabilities of risk-taking behavior in a particular setting. This study, then, chalks one up for the personality, developmental, or intrinsic theory of life-threatening behavior, as contrasted with the environmental—but it is only one study and should not be made to do the work of an entire series.

8. Research of this type does not have to be very expensive; it is often more interesting than paper-and-pencil procedures and computeristic gymnastics; and offers useful training experiences for researchers and clinicians.

REFERENCES

Lester, D. Attitudes toward death today and thirty-five years ago. *Omega,* 1971, 2, 168-173.

Alexander, I., Colley, R. S., and Adlerstein, A. M. Is death a matter of indifference? *J. Psychol.,* 1957, 43, 277-283.

Alexander, I., and Adlerstein, A. M. Death and religion. In H. Feifel (ed.), *The meaning of death.* New York: McGraw-Hill, 1959, 271-283.

Paris, J., and Goodstein, L. D. Responses to death and sex stimulus materials as a function of repression-sensitization. *Psychol. Reports,* 1966, 1283-1291.

Lester, G., and Lester, D. The fear of death, the fear of dying, and threshold differences for death words and neutral words. *Omega,* 1970, 1, 175-180.

Hinton, John. *Dying.* Baltimore, Md.: Pelican, 1970.

Glaser, B. G., and Strauss, A. *Awareness of dying.* Chicago: Aldine, 1965.

Glaser, B. G., and Strauss, A. *Time for dying.* Chicago: Aldine, 1968.

Kubler-Ross, E. *On death and dying.* New York: Macmillan, 1969.

Weisman, A. D. *On dying and denying.* New York: Behavioral Publications, 1972.

Weisman, A. D., and Kastenbaum, R. *The psychological autopsy: A study of the terminal phase of life.* New York: Behavioral Publications, 1968.

Shneidman, E. S. Orientations toward death: A vital aspect of the study of lives. In R. W. White (ed.), *The study of lives.* New York: Atherton Press, 1963, 200-227.

Teahan, J., and Kastenbaum, R. Subjective life expectancy and future time perspective as predictors of job success in the "hard-core unemployed." *Omega,* 1970, 3, 189-200.

Sabatini, P., and Kastenbaum, R. The do-it-yourself death certificate as a research technique. *Life Threatening Behavior,* 1973, 2, 20-32.

CHAPTER
11

The Last Strand:
Remnants of Engagement
in the Later Years[1]

Victor W. Marshall

In this chapter I will examine a group of the aged whose hold on life is somewhat tenuous; they are in many respects highly disengaged from the broader role relationships in which they participated while younger, and they show the characteristic acceptance of death which one might expect among the highly disengaged (Chellam, 1964; Cumming and Henry, 1961). At the same time, however, and coincident with acceptance of death, and even desire to die, these individuals find themselves in a situation where they have good reasons for continued living. They are held to a desire to live by one last strand of engagement, the kinship strand. An examination of these people sheds some light on disengagement theory, but, more important, also on the experience of living while aging and dying.

Data explored here stem from research I have conducted in a retirement village which I have called Glen Brae, and for which I have reported other data elsewhere (Marshall, 1972a, 1972b, 1973, Fall 1973). While gathering these data I also spent time observing and interviewing in a home for the aged which I call St. Joseph's Home. The latter is a lower-class, primarily welfare, home run by a Catholic order of nuns; the former is a middle-to-upper-class non-sectarian community of approximately 400 residents. Both are located in an Eastern seaboard state in the U.S.A. The "last strand" of which I speak in

[1] Prepared for presentation at the Social Science Division sessions of The Canadian Association on Gerontology, Ottawa, Canada, October, 1973.

this chapter is found only in the retirement village, but brief considerations of the home for the aged are introduced for contrast effect.

The verbatim quotations cited in the paper were obtained through informal conversation with residents, but especially in answer to several series of questions dealing with the residents' views of their own anticipated life expectancy, both its estimate and desirability, their assessment of the benefits and dissatisfactions of old age, and their opinions about the appropriateness of death. Two questions in particular were useful in generating the data for these concerns. One asked the individual if he would like to live to be 100 years old. There were none who wished to do so without qualification, and the reasons why they would not prove insightful. The second question asked the individual if he agreed with the statement, "Death always comes too soon." Only 11% of Glen Brae residents felt that death always comes too soon. The remainder offered elaborations suggesting good reasons why death frequently comes too late, or, more rarely, why it can come just in time. As the importance of the "last strand" was not anticipated before I started collecting data, I cannot offer a highly systematic analysis here, but the words of these aging respondents themselves establish the importance of this concept for an understanding of the aging and dying.

THE TENUOUS HOLD ON LIFE

It is argued by disengagement theorists that a benefit of disengagement is that it allows the individual to die without anxiety over unfulfilled plans and projects. Cumming and Henry (1961: 226), for example, suggest that:

> When a middle-aged man dies, he is torn from the fabric of life; when an old man dies, he has already unravelled the web of interaction so much that he can slip from life almost unnoticed. Old people thus feel ready to die, and this may be why . . . they discuss death with considerable poise.

But not all old people are highly disengaged from the "fabric of life," even if their engagement is tenuous. One of the female residents of Glen Brae, asked how old she would like to live to be, expresses this tenuous interest in living: "I wouldn't care if I died tomorrow—if I finished a few things I'd like to do." A male married subject is likewise "ready to go," but "willing to live":

> I have no worry about passing out. You know, that's the least of my troubles. These old ladies here—they talk your head off. I think I've run the end of my rope now—I'm prepared to quit tomorrow if the Good Lord takes me away. My wife and I wouldn't want to live outside of Glen Brae at this period of our lives—not in this cockeyed world.

But it seems he would like just a little time yet. Asked how long he thought he would live, he replied, "If I could live another year, I'll be thankful." To the question "Would you like to live to be 100?" this 93 year old man said he wouldn't mind, "Outside of present aches and pains. I'd like to do some more things—read some books." He did not read many, for this gentleman died a few months later.

Lucas (1968: 8-9; 1969: 248-249) reports data from a study of trapped coal-miners who, upon rescue after from six to eight-and-a-half days, were interviewed as to their thoughts and concerns while in the mine. He found that the threat of premature death caused them concern about short-term unfinished business, such as a planned hunting trip, or plans to pay a minor debt. This is in keeping with a finding by Diggory and Rothman (1961) that, of several reasons why death is "feared," the statement, "All my plans and projects would come to an end," is frequently endorsed by subjects varying in age, sex, religion, social class, and marital status. Diggory (1966: 405) summarizes this study by suggesting that "people fear death because it eliminates opportunities to pursue goals which are important to their self-esteem."

Our data suggest that this conclusion might not apply to the very old, many of whom have no uncompleted plans and projects. Diggory and Rothman did not address themselves to this problem. Their highest age category begins at age 55, and in their sample there was no consistent change by age in the rank-ordering of this statement as a reason for fear.

Unfinished business was not an important reason given for wishing to live longer by our subjects. There were no instances of this reason recorded at St. Joseph's nor at Glen Brae. Outside of some plans by three respondents to write some family history, and a few plans for summer vacations, any other responses which might fit this category can be interpreted merely as a continued zest for living, or as an absence of developed legitimations for dying.

A second reason for living can be provided by an investment of the resident's energies in the retirement community. Particularly at Glen Brae, many residents become involved in the wide range of volunteer activities. It is difficult to identify whether such involvement has the specific function of providing a legitimation for continued living. I judge only one case at St. Joseph's in that light. Although the youngest resident at St. Joseph's, he is prepared to die at any time. In the meantime, however, acting from deep religious concerns, he seems to feel a vocation to visit with other residents and try to keep them happy. Similarly, at Glen Brae, one woman is ready to die "tomorrow, I guess"; but she finds a reason for living in service to other community members, particularly one close friend:

> I hope to be of more use here to people—to residents. Now that really has more meaning to it than I said. There are lots of lonely, unhappy, ill people. And there are a great many things we can do for them. We've just got to be more imaginative. Unlike a town, this is a place where you can really be felt.

With respect to her close friend at Glen Brae:

> I see her as sort of lonely and confused; and life holds very little. I don't want to become involved again, but on the other hand, I try to bring things into her life.

Being involved in the community in this way represents a continuing engagement—or, more precisely, a re-engagement in the new residential setting, suggesting a reluctance to just sit back and "slip away from the fabric of life." Retirement communities and other congregate facilities for the aging can offer such opportunities for maintaining the hold on life which might be less available in the wider community (Aldridge, 1956; Atlas and Morris, 1970; Granick, 1957; Hochschild, 1973; Hoyt, 1954; Kalson, 1972; Kleemeier, 1954; Perrow and Sequin, 1972; Rosow, 1962). The investment of one's commitments in voluntary activities and community life in congregate residential facility for the aging can provide limited substitutes for the decreased role-engagement which accompanies the aging process. A subset of the aging, however, whether in a congregate facility or not, are characterized by a continuity of the kinship role, which becomes the major focus of their continued living, and the last remaining important strand linking them to life, and causing them to wish that their death, however acceptable to them eventually, will be put off for just a while. They continue living "for each other."

THE LAST STRAND

"Living for each other" represents a continued state of engagement which provides a legitimation for desiring to live longer. Here the evidence is very clear as to the significance of this engagement, because in numerous interviews respondents argued their willingness, even anxiousness to die but for the one reason that they must continue to live for the sake of a specific other. This occurred only at Glen Brae, and within kinship groupings, particularly marriage. The type of legitimation is, however, most poignantly illustrated by a woman, age 96, who lives at Glen Brae with her sister, who is 90. She told me about a dream she had, mentioning it on two interviews over a time-interval of more than a month:

> I dreamed that I knocked at the door—St. Peter's—and I said, "St. Peter, let me in." And he said, "No. Go back, you're needed." And I did.

An examination of the elder sister's answers to several questions shows this to be a continuing concern. Asked how old she would like to live to be, she replied:

> I'd like to live as old as I am useful. And after that I'm perfectly willing to go. I told you St. Peter wouldn't let me in.

Would she agree that "death is sometimes a blessing"?

> Oh. Well, if I were dependent upon anybody, then I would say it was a blessing. But no, I don't think it's a blessing. I agree with St. Peter—that I'm needed.

At the end of the series of three interviews, the elder sister commented again on her dream:

> My dream—it bothered me to think that I was doing so little. I decided I could be spared and asked St. Peter to let me in. He said "No—you're needed. Go back to where you came from." A silly dream. I'm glad that I'm physically able and mentally able to do things. I'm very grateful for the whole thing. I don't know how my sister could get along without me and how I could get along without her.

Note in these quotations that the respondent is concerned that she continue to be useful—particularly to her younger sister. She, in fact, views death as being "spared" the misfortune of not being useful enough. But St. Peter tells her (you make your own "analysis"; the material is clear to me) she is in fact still useful and still needed. For this she is grateful. She knows her sister cannot get along without her. This gives her a reason for living.

The elder sister recognized that just as her younger sister needs her, she needs her sister. It is thus interesting to note that the younger, though with less elaboration, employs the same legitimation for living.

Q. "How old would you like to live to be?"
A. "When I'm no use to my sister any longer. Physically I'm more useless than she is."

Both sisters estimate that they will live "a couple of years" longer.

Living for each other is not always reciprocal; nor, when it is, is this always recognized. An 86-year-old male resident of Glen Brae would like to live "as long as I can to take care of these two ladies (wife and sister-in-law). After they pass on I have nothing else to live for particularly." A widow does not want to live to be 100, "But I hope the Good Lord lets me live to outlive my daughter (an invalid). I know she doesn't know why she's alive." Asked what in her life today gives her the most happiness, she cites making her daughter happy. Another sister pair reflects the "living for another" theme. One sister would like to live "As long as I'm well. And really—I have a provision to that—long enough to take care of my sister. She's 94" (respondent is 79).

An 87 year old male would like to live:

> . . . as long as my wife does—longer, 'cause I want to look after her. Outside of that, I think I'm old enough. I mean you lose your outlook on life to some extent, realize your time is limited.

He says he would not like to live to 100, because "I haven't enough life in me." Death is a blessing "For the person who dies, if he lives long enough. I wouldn't say it was a blessing for anyone else."

A female resident says "If I were to die tomorrow, I would suffer mentally, knowing I leave a husband who loved and needed me in several ways." One gets the impression from some cases that both parties to a marriage legitimate further living only for the sake of their spouse. The following cases, with husband and wife interviewed separately, illustrate this: The wife:

> I really worry about the fact that I should go first, if I do. Because I could weather it better than he could. . . . When I was down in the infirmary he got the notion I wasn't well. He never showed it to me. (Two ministers) said my husband was in a flap.

The husband, when asked when he imagined people think most about death, said:

> I never gave it a thought myself. I just live in the present. It's true recently I wondered what would happen if I should pass on and leave my wife with nobody . . . (later) If I should pass on, my wife will be in one awful state because of her condition (a serious disease).

For some of the residents at Glen Brae, living in the retirement community is related to this "living for each other." We earlier discussed a male respondent, now deceased, whose only reason for living had been a desire to read a few more books. He had praised Glen Brae, the general life there, but especially its medical facilities. His wife, on the other hand, described the move to Glen Brae as "the final, not quite final," turning point in her life. Asked if it was a good turning point, she said, "sensible, but not pleasant." A male subject (who has in fact since left Glen Brae) also claimed to have moved to Glen Brae because of his wife's health:

> When I had this so-called heart attack, it occurred to me what would happen to her if I wasn't here to look after her. If it happened here, there would be some rallying around on the part of the people in the corridor. And the management would take care of her.

> [later] The reason I came to Glen Brae was clearly because of my wife's condition. And I was of the opinion that she would have excellent care here if she had to have it for an extended period of time. She was told two years ago that she had three months. She's still alive. Part of it is she has no worries. If it were me alone, I wouldn't be here.

Thus, the "living for each other" theme affects the life-style of some of the aged. For some couples, living at Glen Brae offers an adventitious form of living together and for each other while under threat of impending death. As another resident put it, when asked how he would change his life right now, if he could, "I'd—I don't think I would. I'd give my wife good health and go live in a house of our own."

This form of legitimation for continued living affects only a small proportion of Glen Brae residents, but enough to make it worthy of note. In sharper focus, it can be seen when such legitimation is absent. As one widow expressed her greatest disappointment: "My husband's death. It changed the whole world for me. He wished we could die together, and I do too." Just as life with the spouse of several decades can legitimate continued living, life without can legitimate dying:

Q. "If you were going to live your life over again, what would you change?"
A. "Well I'd have me die before my husband. Let me die first."
Q. "What do you hope to accomplish in your future?"
A. "To die before my family [i.e., children] do."

And another:

Q. "What in your life gives you the greatest feeling of disappointment?"
A. "That my husband didn't live on with me. It's too bad husbands and wives can't die together."

Indeed, some evidence is beginning to accumulate that when the last strand is broken, death may be precipitated. Several observers have pointed to the increased incidence of death among widows and widowers (Parkes, 1972; Parkes, Benjamin and Fitzgerald, 1969; Rees and Lutkins, 1967; Young, Benjamin and Wallis, 1963). Parkes, noting that about three-quarters of the increased death rate among the bereaved was attributable to coronary thrombosis, arteriosclerotic heart disease, and other types of heart disease (Parkes, 1972: 16), has utilized the term, "the broken heart syndrome" to describe a process which, though little understood in its dynamics, has been referred to in common parlance for centuries. The converse of dying from a broken heart might well be the "living for each other" which I have described above. The work of David Phillips (1969; Koenig, 1972), which suggests that many individuals can postpone the time of their deaths in order to live to witness important events (birthdays, anniversaries, the Jewish Day of Atonement, Presidential elections) is probably also relevant here. I do not have appropriate data to assess whether my subjects are living longer than might be expected actuarily, or whether they die unexpectedly following the death of the other, but the sentiments expressed by them are suggestive as to the ways in which the "last strand" could have these effects.

THE VITAL BALANCE

With respect to the "reasons for living" discussed above, we must bear in mind their place in the phenomenal world of the aging. Many old people, at least many of those in this study, have highly-developed legitimations for their own impending death (Marshall, 1972a, 1972b, 1973). These may or may not be accompanied by legitimations for continued living. Peter Berger and Thomas Luckmann (1967: 101) argue that "it is in the legitimation of death that the transcending potency of symbolic universes manifests itself most clearly ..." Berger (1969) in particular argues for the importance of religion in this regard. Here I would like to suggest that the "reasons for living" we have discussed indicate that the "good death" for some at least can come from living out a legitimated life in maintaining self-esteem through realizing one's projects (Diggory and Rothman, 1961; Diggory, 1966), in living for the others in one's community, and in living for a particular other. The symbolic construction of a "good death"—one that is seen as appropriate and legitimate—reflects then a delicate counterpoise between legitimation of one's life and legitimation of death itself.

One of the older residents of Glen Brae is a spinster, age 91, who has greatly enjoyed the more than thirty years of her retirement, does not want to live to be 100 years old. "But," she says, "I'm having a good time so I'm not ready yet."

Legitimations for death can thus co-exist with legitimations for continued living, held in reserve, so to speak, for when they will be needed. A woman with persistent physical pain says:

> I don't have very many good days, but still I don't feel as if I'm ready to go for a while. But once I get helpless, I wouldn't want to live. See, I can dress myself and take care of myself. I'm very fortunate in having a very good kind husband.

As a major frustration of growing older, another respondent lists the "infirmities of age":

> But I'm not worried about it. I was going to say, "If I die when I should." My friend said, "I have enough china to last—if I die when I oughta."

So long as the possibility of an intelligible life exists, the reasons for dying can be held in abeyance, for use when necessary. People can be at the same time, however, quite ready to die, as is exemplified by a woman who says:

> This is a lucky age. It's awfully nice to grow old, I think. Health is the crux. And not too many regrets. Regrets are killing.

This illustrates the two-fold nature of legitimation, giving legitimation for death and for life, for this respondent is "ready to pass on any time now." If her health continues, however, she is quite happy to live:

> I think (I'd like to live to) 88. I'd be quite ready to go at 88, but I change every year. Next year I might be (saying) 89. As you get older you want to live longer.

As she gets older, this respondent wants to continue living—but only if her health continues. If her health fails, she is *now* quite ready to die. The possession at the same time of legitimations for living and for dying is illustrated most adequately (and most poignantly) in the case of those who are ready to die but for the responsibility of the care of another, as we have noted above.

Reasons for living are related to the projecting of the self into the future, through planning and anticipation. But there is, for some, a more fundamental dimension to the legitimation of continued life. As literature on suicide

(Douglas, 1967; Henslin, 1970; Jacobs, 1970) demonstrates, continued living is not problematical for the young, and needs no legitimation vis-à-vis the alternative of dying, which does. In a society where aging and being old is devalued by many, including the aged themselves (Rosow, 1967: 30-35), this devaluation must surely call to account, for many, their very existence. Reasons for living must be very good reasons in the face of the widely-held belief that the aged are socially useless. Thus, one female resident said, "My general feeling is that people live far too long"; and, indicating that she herself was very close to death by placing her mark on a line drawn between the words Life and Death said, "I hope I'm about there.... Yes, I hope so ..."

For another, death does not come too soon for those suffering, but also for those who are very old:

> I've heard any number of people say, "You can live too long." And they mean it from the bottom of their hearts.

Another subject thinks death can be a blessing for the surviving children: ". . . often a parent will live long and hold a child down and keep the child to them." This widow does not want to live any longer: "I don't want to live in this world any more than I have to."

Even at Glen Brae, where residents are self-sufficient and pay their own way, some feel that their very continued existence is called into account by others. At St. Joseph's Home, where most are on welfare, we would expect this feeling to be even more prevalent. One day there had been a funeral in the morning at St. Joseph's, and at lunch one of the men spontaneously brought up the topic of death. He said:

> I was talking with a guy this morning and I said, "When you get 70, you should die." He said no, he wanted to live. I said, "What for? You produce anything? You bring home bread and butter? Better you die."

CONCLUSION

In the future, the importance of the "last strand" is likely to decline, because of shifts in death rate. The aged themselves are getting older. United States government projections indicate that although the population aged 65 and over will increase 50% between 1960 and 1985, the population over age 85 will nearly double. But more of these aged will be women, and hence most will be widows. While women 65-plus now outnumber men 134 to 100, by 1985 the ratio will probably be about 150-100 (all figures from U.S. Senate, 1969: 3). If living with and for another is a "last strand" holding many people to life, we will find that, for most, the last strand will be broken. We are likely to find ourselves (and I literally mean ourselves, because many of us will be either dead or close to it when these projections have been realized) in a situation where we have no longer any reason for living, no last strand.

Disengagement theory has a great deal to tell us about the process of severing ties with society, and its recommendation is that a voluntary acceptance of disengagement will lead to high levels of satisfaction. Paradoxically, though disengagement is held to be precipitated by awareness of impending death (Cumming and Henry, 1961: 224; Damianopoulos, 1961: 216-217), and while it focuses on the severing of role relationships, we find little in the work of the disengagement theorists concerning the very last strand of engagement, and the experience of severing that strand. Perhaps this is because of the tendency of disengagement theorists to measure engagement and disengagement via the abstractions of role-counts and social life-space measures. Perhaps we have to listen more closely to the aging individual himself concerning the importance of his life with others, particularly those others who are closest to him, and for whom he wishes to continue to live; and perhaps we have to attend more systematically, and sympathetically, to the severing of the last strand.

REFERENCES

Aldridge, Gordon: The Role of Older People in a Florida Retirement Community. *Geriatrics 11*: 223-226, 1956.

Atlas, L., and Morris, M.: Resident Government: an Instrument for Change in a Public Institution for Indigent Elderly. Paper presented at the 23rd Annual Meeting of the Gerontological Society. Toronto, Canada, 1970.

Berger, Peter: *The Sacred Canopy*. Garden City: Doubleday Anchor, 1969.

____, and Luckmann, Thomas: *The Social Construction of Reality*. Garden City: Doubleday Anchor, 1967.

Chellam, Grace: *The Disengagement Theory: Awareness of Death and Self-Engagement*. D.S.W. Thesis, Western Reserve University, 1964.

Cumming, E., and Henry, Wm.: *Growing old, the Process of Disengagement*. New York: Basic Books, 1961.

Damianopoulos, E.: A Formal Statement of Disengagement Theory. Ch. XII, pp. 210-218, in E. Cumming and Wm. Henry, *Growing Old, the Process of Disengagement*. New York: Basic Books, 1961.

Diggory, James: *Self-Evaluation: Concepts and Studies*. New York: John Wiley and Sons, 1966.

____, and Rothman, D.: Values Destroyed by Death. *Journal of Abnormal and Social Psychology 63*: 205-210, 1961.

Douglas, Jack: *The Social Meaning of Suicide*. Princeton: Princeton University Press, 1967.

Granick, S.: Personality Adjustment of the Aged in Retirement Communities. *Geriatrics 12*: 381-285, 1957.

Henslin, J.: Guilt and Guilt Neutralization: Response and Adjustment to Suicide. Ch. 7, pp. 192-228, in J. Douglas (Ed.), *Deviance and Respectability*. New York: Basic Books, 1970.

Hochschild, Arlie: *The Unexpected Community*. Englewood Cliffs: Prentice-Hall, 1973.

Hoyt, G. C.: The Life of the Retired in a Trailer Park. *American Journal of Sociology 59*: 361-370, 1954.

Jacobs, J.: The Use of Religion in Constructing the Moral Justification of Suicide. Ch. 8, pp. 229-251, in J. Douglas (Ed.), *Deviance and Respectability*. New York: Basic Books, 1970.

Kalson, Leon: The Therapy of Independent Living for the Elderly. *Journal of the American Geriatrics Society 20*: 394-397, 1972.

Kleemeier, Robert: Moosehaven: Congregate Living in a Community of the Retired. *American Journal of Sociology 59*: 347-351, 1954.

Koenig, Peter, Death Doth Defer. *Psychology Today 6*, no. 6 (November): 83, 1972.

Lucas, Rex: Social Implications of the Immediacy of Death. *The Canadian Review of Sociology and Anthropology 5*: 1-16, 1968.

____, *Men in Crisis*. New York: Basic Books, 1969.

Marshall, Victor W.: Continued Living and Dying as Problematical Aspects of Old Age: an Empirical Study. Paper presented at the IX International Congress of Gerontology, Kiev, U.S.S.R., 1972a.

____, *Continued Living and Dying as Problematical Aspects of Old Age*. Unpublished Doctoral Dissertation, Department of Sociology, Princeton University, 1972b.

____, Awareness of Finitude and Developmental Theory in Gerontology: Some Speculations. Paper presented for the Berkeley Conference on Death and Dying, Berkeley, California, 1973.

____, Game-Analyzable Dilemmas in a Retirement Village: a Case Study. *Aging and Human Development*, 4(4), Fall 1973.

Parkes, C. M.: *Bereavement: Studies of Grief in Adult Life*. New York: International Universities Press, 1972.

____, Benjamin, B., and Fitzgerald, R. G.: Broken Heart: a Statistical Study of Increased Mortality among Widowers. *British Medical Journal 1*: 740, 1969.

Perrow, B. C., and Seguin, M. M.: Resident Life Experience as Influenced by Perceptions of Structure in Four Retirement Homes. Paper presented at the 25th Annual Meeting of the Gerontological Society, San Juan, Puerto Rico, 1972.

Phillips, David P.: *Dying as a Form of Social Behavior*. Unpublished Doctoral Thesis, Department of Sociology, Princeton University, 1969.

Rees, W. D., and Lutkins, S. G.: Mortality of Bereavement. *British Medical Journal 4:* 13-16, 1967.

Rosow, Irving: Retirement Housing and Social Integration, pp. 327-340 in Tibbitts, C., and Donahue, W. (Eds.), *Social and Psychological Aspects of Aging*. New York: Columbia University Press, 1962.

____, *Social Integration of the Aged*. New York: Free Press, 1967.

United States Senate, Special Committee on Aging: *Economics of Aging: Toward a Full Share in Abundance, a Working Paper*. Washington: U.S. Govt. Printing Office, 1969.

Young, M., Benjamin, B., and Wallis, C.: Mortality of Widowers. *Lancet 2*: 454, 1963.

CHAPTER
12

Old People
Talk About:
The Right to Die*

Shura Saul
and
Sidney R. Saul

Background

The right to die is not a new issue — but one with a long history of philosophical
and ethical scrutiny. Neither entrance to — nor exit from life — is controlled by
the individual within his own vital processes.

This very fact highlights the dilemma of an individual's freedom within his
social structure. Society refuses a person the right to exercise choices regarding
his own exodus from this world. Instead, society sends out a double message.
On the one hand it is illegal to perform an act of violence, homicide or suicide.
On the other, the state reserves the right to take a person's life (as punishment
for certain crimes). On a mass scale, in the name of national security, carnage,
violence and homicide are legitimized under the heading of war. In some
circumstances even the suicide of able bodied, mentally alert persons is expected
and encouraged — as in the case of intelligence agents who are issued suicide kits.

Apparently, when it suits certain purposes of the power structure — certain
kinds of killing can be accepted as moral and ethical. However, an individual's
right and power to make similar decisions for himself creates conflicts in the
very same society.

All of these concepts were brought to open social awareness in the recent case
of Karen Quinlan, whose hovering between life and death engaged the attention
of many people, including older persons living in institutionalized settings.

Death is a constant presence for older persons who live in an institution.

* A Discussion prompted by the Karen Quinlan Case (held at the Kingsbridge Heights
Manor, Bronx, New York).

When as many as 200 sick, old people live under one roof, death becomes a fact of life — a weekly, if not a daily occurrence.

One of the "life tasks" of the elderly individual is to face the imminence of his own death, and to cope with it in some way. Many older people talk about it, "put their house in order," in tangible ways, some draft a will, or give away possessions; in less tangible ways, some reminisce, etc. Those older people for whom institutionalized living has become the only way to spend their last few years (usually without alternative) often become depressed and express a death wish, a desire to "just pass away"; some even threaten suicide. Such a threat may really be another way of expressing dissatisfaction with life: a wish to "have it all over and done with," and a desire to control, at least, ending their life process over which there is so little control at this point.

Many persons feel they already died when circumstances over which they had no control ultimately mandated institutionalization.

The group participating in the discussion recorded as follows, consists of some such people. They are among the most active, verbal, angry and disgruntled residents in a 200-bed H.R.F.[1] Persons who live with anger and fear about which they can do precious little are prime candidates for severe depression; older persons in this state may develop senile psychosis and other forms of mental illness.

In the institution, intervention to prevent this becomes a major activity and a crucial goal. One valuable interventive modality is the group process. The staff group psychotherapist was therefore asked to develop a group for some people who were mostly "loners" in the Home. A primary purpose of the group is to offer an opportunity to express the anger, the fear and frustration of these residents about their present living arrangement. It was hoped that they could thereby come to some terms with it.

The discussion about the "Right to Die" came up as a "natural motivational situation." At the prior meeting there had been a meaningful discussion on the nature of group living and life in the institution; its losses, gains and personalities, and so forth.

Finally, the discussion drifted on to reveal the feelings of some residents as "no longer wanting to live," because of their current circumstances. The issue of suicide was verbalized by Mrs. Lillian who stated . . . "No one has the right to take some one else's life — but his own life is his business!" This prompted Mr. Harold to comment — "There is this girl, she's really dead, all the doctors and tests say she's dead, but they are keeping her 'alive' with machines! There is nothing there, why keep her alive?"

There was an immediate intense response pro and con. Since it was getting late, the leader suggested that this discussion be continued next time. In preparation, the people were encouraged to read and listen to the news about

[1] Health Related Facility (H.R.F.) — An H.R.F. is a residential setting for people requiring some assistance and supervision in many activities of daily living, but who do not require skilled nursing care around the clock.

the Quinlan girl. They agreed with anticipation. This in itself, being future-oriented, encouraged an interest in living.

Group Discussion

Participants in group:

Mr. Harold — 78	Mr. Lillian — over 80
Mr. Arthur — 81	Walters, M.D. — 62
Mr. Jackson — 60	Mr. Thor — 71
Mrs. Lillian — over 70	Mr. Philips — 74

Leader: Dr. Sidney R. Saul, Ed.D., C.S.W. — age 55

I introduced the tape recorder and asked the residents' permission. They granted it:

Dr. Saul:　　I'd like to pick up where we left off last time. Does anyone recall?

Mr. Lillian:　About the girl?

Dr. Saul:　　Perhaps we could focus on the Quinlan case. Does the person or the family have the right to say "let her die?"

Mr. Lillian:　Any person has the right to die.

Mr. Thor:　　Do you mean the "right" or the "say" in whether they are to die or not?

Dr. Saul:　　O.K. Do they have the right to have the say?

Mr. Thor:　　Yes, they do.

Mr. Jackson:　*And how* they do have that right! If a person wants to die, why not? If he has a terminal illness — absolutely! Why should he suffer the rest of his life?

Mr. Thor:　　She is in no condition to decide whether she wants to live or not.

Mr. Harold:　Just a second. That party who is involved can't talk in the court room. So the question is whether the parents have the right to decide. Do they have the right to say, "Please pull the plug out and let her die in peace?" That is the question.

Mr. Thor:　　Nobody has the right to take her life no matter what condition she's in. They did not give her life — they can't take it away.

Mr. Jackson:　Are you talking about the religious aspects?

Mr. Thor:　　No! Leave her alone — she's going to die naturally. Anyone who takes his own life is committing suicide and it's their own responsibility. But here, someone has to take the life.

Dr. Saul:	*There are some complications* — does anyone want to answer Mr. Thor?
Mr. Jackson:	Yes, the child will be a burden for the rest of her life!
Mr. Thor:	A child is a burden under any circumstances, isn't it?
Mr. Jackson:	She's going to die anyway!
Dr. Saul:	Mr. Thor, if the only way this girl can remain alive is by being hooked up to a machine — does that make a difference? If the prognosis was she could live another 50 years on a machine — would you still feel the way you do?
Mr. Thor:	Yes, why not? You have no right to take the life. Medical progress might find a way. If you pull the plug there is no hope for anybody.
Mrs. Lillian:	I think that if a person is that sick, she has a right to die.
Dr. Saul:	But she has no brain, so she can't make her own decision.
Mr. Harold:	The parents should decide.
Mr. Lillian:	If she has parents, can the parents say "pull the plug?" — No, it's her own life — the parents have no right. It's her own life. If she does not say so, you cannot do it. How can the parents say she must die? Say there is a fellow that's crazy and another fellow comes over and says he must die — where are you? For instance, I'm sick and my parents say "he's sick, let him die" — that's not right.
Dr. Saul:	Let us take you as an example. If you discovered you have a terminal illness and you have two weeks to live and that it will be very, very painful for you — do you have the right to say "Don't give me medication, don't put me on a machine, let me die."
Mr. Lillian:	Yes, I have the right.
Dr. Saul:	Now suppose you go into a coma — you lose consciousness. You still will die in two weeks but your body goes through a great deal of torment — they can keep you alive with a machine. Would you want your wife to be able to say, "Don't put him on a machine?"
Mr. Lillian:	Yes, that's right, yes.
Dr. Saul:	That is what we are discussing here about the Quinlan case.
Walters, M.D.:	It's been months — 6 months of deterioration. There is nothing left — let her die.
Dr. Saul:	If you read carefully to see how she became so ill — one realizes she took an overdose of pills mixed with alcohol and that this is the result of a suicide attempt.

Mr. Harold: Yes, she took pills and alcohol.

Mr. Jackson: What? I didn't know that.

Mr. Lillian: Then she said it herself — she wants to die — so she should be allowed to die.

Mr. Thor: But they caught her and she didn't die.

Mr. Harold: When she was in her full mind she took all that junk. The question is now while she is in a coma, have we got the right to end her life. In some states it's legal, in others illegal. In the future I believe it will be legal everywhere anyway. That's the progress of civilization.

Mr. Jackson: It will become legal in time.

Dr. Saul: What about for yourself?

Mr. Jackson: I would want the right to say I want to die. To say that's all, I had it.

Mrs. Lillian: The same.

(All in the room agree they want that right for themselves.)

Mr. Harold: If I am incurable and very sick — I want to be done with it, I want to die. I'd want to kill myself altogether.

Mr. Philips: I don't know, there's a big confusion here. It isn't the question whether you want to die or whether you don't want to die. The party in the condition in which they are now, has no common sense and does not know what to say — whether they want to die or do not want to die. So you are really talking about the people that are near and dear to the person who is sick. The fact is whether they want to.

Walters, M.D.: The parents claim that if she knew she was a vegetable and incurable she would not want to be kept alive. Also, if you had a daughter who for 6 months has been on a machine — everything says she's dead, she's down to 60 lbs. The brain waves show that her brain is already dead. Would you want her to live?

Mr. Philips: Still you wouldn't want to give that up.

Mr. Lillian: I don't understand. For instance, if I took something to kill me and I was asked do I want to live and I say "yes" or "no" — no one has the right to interfere — it's my life — that's my opinion.

Dr. Saul: That opens up another question. I work in a mental hospital and we have a crisis intervention program. If someone attempts to commit suicide, we go out and get them without their permission, we will pump stomachs and do everything we can to keep them alive.

Mr. Lillian: Sure, this is the proper way. But for instance, I want to die.

Dr. Saul: Under what circumstances?

Mr. Lillian: It doesn't matter what circumstances. I'm old and I'm tired of life and I want to commit suicide. If I try, of course the doctor has to try and save me! He can't say, "Let him die." You know what I mean?

Mr. Harold: For your information, let me straighten it out — if you want to commit suicide, it's against the law, you know that.

Dr. Saul: When you get to heaven, they will arrest you!
. . . (laughter)

Mr. Lillian: It's against the law to commit suicide, it's against the law to steal too — but people do it all the time!

Dr. Saul: When we talk about a 20-year-old, healthy young man — who gets very depressed and takes an overdose of pills and wants to die — the hospital says he does not have the right to make that decision and we keep him alive.

Mr. Lillian: That is different. If he does it, the doctor should try to save him.

Dr. Saul: We do more than that — we put him in the hospital and prevent him from killing himself.

Mr. Lillian: That is a different story.

Dr. Saul: But — if a person has a terminal illness and if left alone might live two weeks or two months but the living will be very painful, very bad. If at that point, the person says, "I want to die, don't give me medication, don't put me on a machine, let me die sooner rather than later."

Mr. Lillian: If he says so and expresses himself that way, it means he consents.

Dr. Saul: Do you see that as different from a person who is only depressed and is healthy in all other ways and tries to kill himself — what should we do?

Mr. Lillian: No, that person should not be allowed to die.

Mr. Arthur: What is the question now?

Dr. Saul: We are discussing whether the Quinlan parents have the right to make the decision.

Mr. Harold: We don't have the right to think anything about them.

Mr. Lillian: (Angrily) — Well, who does.

Mr. Harold:	That has to be left up to God Himself.
Mr. Jackson:	Wait a minute, now hold it. What do you mean God Himself? God has nothing to do with this.
Mr. Philips:	He's an atheist, that is why he says that.
Mr. Thor:	God didn't devise the machines.
Mr. Harold:	Well, I'll tell you something — as far as I can recollect, God has never put Himself in anybody's position. He put him here to do what he has to. He will not tell you what to do.
Dr. Saul:	What is the position of the church in the Quinlan case? This is a very devout Catholic family — what does the church say?
Mr. Thor:	Not to pull the plug?
Walters, M.D.:	The church says, let God decide. The machines are not God — the doctors say she will no longer live if they are cut off. She cannot live under any circumstances as she is too deteriorated. So they say — if God wishes to create a miracle, then He will; if not, she'll die, whichever is His will! As long as she is in the machine, God cannot handle it, the machine handles it.
Mr. Jackson:	That's a bunch of malarky.
Walters, M.D.:	Jack, I don't think you heard what I said. I said the church said you can remove her from the machine.
Mr. Jackson:	Oh, in that case, O.K.
Mr. Harold:	She's dead already. It's only a machine that keeps her alive. Just take her out and let her die. She has no brains, nothing. It's not a question of God or religion, it's a question of parent's rights in this case.
Mr. Jackson:	I applaud you for that!
Mr. Harold:	A question of legality is also involved — what is the law?
Mr. Lillian:	No matter what it is; a machine, a human being, anything living is controlled by God. If God didn't want a machine, there would be no machine.
Dr. Saul:	O.K. Let me raise another problem: If you were the judge, on what basis would you make your decision, whatever that decision is? What factors would you consider?
Walters, M.D.:	I would take into account the parent's wishes, the condition of the patient (which is one of complete hopelessness), and give the

parents the permission to order the removal of the machines if they so desire. Then if by some miracle she persists in living, she will live — but the odds are a million to one she'll die.*

Mr. Thor: I'd take into account that perhaps the background which created this situation — for example, weakness in her physical structure (was she sick before?) — the complete history of her life, her medical and psychological history.

Dr. Saul: What about the parent's wishes?

Mr. Thor: They decided to have the child. It seems they are sorry they had this child!

Dr. Saul: Do you think the parents would have wanted the child to die 5 years ago.

Mr. Thor: I guess not.

Dr. Saul: Would you take into account the position of the church?

Mr. Thor: Well, you'd have to.

Dr. Saul: Why would you have to?

Mr. Thor: Well, you can't leave it up to the family alone. Even if they were not religious, you'd have to have something outside of the family to guide you.

Mr. Lillian: I would consider the questions in this way. If I wanted to die, that's my business. If God wanted to save me, He'd cause the doctors to help me. They wouldn't recognize my decision otherwise.

Mrs. Lillian: I'm all mixed up. I don't know what to believe, what to think. If the person wants to die, he has a right to it.

Mr. Arthur: (with increasing anger) — let me start with this man here (pointing a finger at Harry S.) — the person doesn't know if she's alive or dead — doesn't know what day it is. He doesn't know anything, not a Goddamn thing about what's going on around him. The machine can go for 20 years and he can live. If the machine is stopped he'd live for 24 hours at most. I say, pull that plug out!

Dr. Saul: As the judge, what factors would you consider — not your decision, but the factors?

Mr. Arthur: Let the parents have the right; they should listen to the doctors. Let me make this short and sweet — pull the plug out! (with anger.) You say the parents are religious, let the church decide.

*EDITOR'S NOTE: As is now well-known, Karen Quinlan did survive the removal of the machines.

Dr. Saul: Is that enough?

(At this point, Mr. Arthur gets very angry and spews out his answers — saying he does not want to consider anything else!)

Mr. Philips: The decision is a very hard one. There are smarter people than us sitting at the conference table and they couldn't come to a conclusion. It's a very touchy thing. You can holler, "pull the plug!" — "don't pull the plug" — church; here — there . . . If you have a belief, all right. No matter what I say, it could be wrong.

I'd consider the amount of suffering and the doctor's ability to cure her. If all get together, church, family and doctors and then decide together. As a judge I would ask them to make the decision.

Mr. Arthur: How many of you have known in your lives — if a child is born and in two or three years the doctors can tell he's a vegetable?

Dr. Saul: Are you talking of a case you know personally?

Mr. Arthur: Yes, it happened to a friend of mine. I used to cut the child's hair, he could not go to a barber. For 20 years he was a vegetable, nothing was there, he was a complete burden to his parents. What would you do in such a case?

Dr. Saul: O.K. — Now we have a real case to look at, something Mr. Arthur has experienced himself. We have a live functioning growing human being who is severely retarded.

Mr. Arthur: (his anger reaching a high pitch) — He can do nothing (he shouts) — nothing! He can't dress, he can't feed himself, he cannot even go to the toilet! Nothing! Nothing! Nothing!

Dr. Saul: Why are you so angry, Mr. Arthur?

Mr. Arthur: I'm not angry! (in a loud and explosive tone.)

Mr. Jackson: I'd say, "Pull the plug and that's the end." I would put him to death.

Dr. Saul: Now we are in a different ball park and it's another game. Do we have the right to put away an individual who is a complete vegetable, who is kept alive by people not by a machine?

Mr. Jackson: (then recounts his experience at the Vets Hospital where a vet was kept alive and in a coma by a machine for 8 years; he could do nothing for himself and finally died.)

They should have pulled the plug 8 years before.

Mr. Philips:	I wouldn't pass an opinion.
Mr. Harold:	This is a new case entirely, I don't want to talk about it. It's against the law to do it. Some day it will be lawful, but not now.
Mr. Thor:	You have no right to make such a law. God won't approve of it.
Mr. Philips:	The situation has to do with the right to take any person's life, it's a hard decision.

(At this point, Arthur returns to the case he raised (with fury and anger) and asks the others what they would do.)

Mr. Lillian:	You want my opinion? I say let him live! He was born to live.
Mr. Jackson:	No, he was not born to live — No, nobody is born to live.
Mr. Lillian:	You were born to live, too.
Mrs. Lillian:	I agree with Harry — for once I agree with my husband! (general laughter)
Mr. Arthur:	(again jumps in with fury and anger) — After 21 years, the father died because he was so heartbroken.
Mr. Lillian:	It makes no difference, the child should live.
Mr. Arthur:	You never had it (angrily) so what do you know.
Dr. Saul:	We have another issue. If the parent is to die early in life due to the aggravation of raising a child who is a complete vegetable, does this change the situation?
Mr. Thor:	There is a difference between a person dying in his 40's and a person dying in his 80's.
Mr. Harold:	The parent should not die, he has a right to live!
Dr. Saul:	What would you do?
Mr. Arthur:	I would send the child to an institution when two or three years old and forget about it. I'd not kill him. I'd let them study him to help other people, but I would not kill him; but I would not wait 20 years.

(Arthur goes on and the rest of his story is told with a softening of tone and tears in his voice as well as eyes.)

And here's another thing. My daughter-in-law's mother (pause) she had cancer. I just saw her at a party and she died the following week. She died and she did not let them give her medicine or machines.

Mr. Jackson: (also with great emotion) — My friend's mother had breast cancer and they wanted to remove the breast. She said, "No," and she died anyhow. They should have taken her breast off and maybe she would have lived! (He wipes away a tear.) Yet I feel she made the right decision.

Mr. Harold: You should have mercy on a person who is in pain and incurable. We have to have mercy. Some day it will be legal, not like now. I want the judge to have mercy and change the law!

Mr. Thor: What will you do with the tape? Will you go to another group with it?

The session is effectively stopped!

PART 3
Transcending Death

Whether you prefer the concept of reincarnation, immortality, life after death, or continuity, you have undoubtedly given some thought to what happens to a person (that is, to you) after clinical death. You may have developed a strong, coherent belief as to what happens, or you may be uncertain; your belief may be unquestioned by you or constantly questioned by you. In one way or another, the issue is an on-going part of your life.

There are many ways to transcend death. Noyes and Kletti have worked with materials nearly a century old, reporting on what happens to people who fall to their death (or almost-death). These people seem to have transcended the dying process in an almost mystical fashion. Their altered states of consciousness remind us of altered states developed through drugs and in other ways, and the various ways undoubtedly have a common base.

Lifton is less descriptive and more theoretical. He explores the entire background of immortality and the continuity of life, showing the diverse ways in which continuity can be achieved. It isn't that the dying process is aided or hindered by the specific view a person takes, but that the dying process — and indeed the rest of our life — is influenced by such feelings. And finally, ending the section and the book, a brief . . . essay? Story? Case study? Anyway, it is brief and very personal.

CHAPTER 13

The Experience
of Dying from Falls

Russell Noyes, Jr. and Roy Kletti

The experience of dying has been neglected in the scientific literature. Jaspers, in his comprehensive *General Psychopathology* (1963), noted that the phenomena experienced by individuals who narrowly escaped death were often discussed but rarely reported. The accounts of persons who have nearly died are limited almost entirely to autobiographical and fictional sources. Jung's (1961) account of his experience immediately following a heart attack and Caresse Crosby's (1953) description of nearly drowning at age seven are dramatic autobiographical examples. Poe's "A Descent into the Maelstrom" (1938) and Ambrose Bierce's "An Occurrence at Owl Creek Bridge" (1920) are representative of fictional accounts.

The first known study of this subject was undertaken by Zurich geology professor Albert Heim (1892) who assiduously collected the subjective observations of survivors of falls in the Alps. He presented his findings before the Uto Section of the Swiss Alpine Club on February 26, 1892. They were subsequently published under the title "Notizen über den Tod durch Absturz" (Remarks on fatal falls) in the Yearbook of the Swiss Alpine Club (Vol. 27, pp. 327-337, Bern, 1892). A true scientist, Heim avoided speculative interpretation of these reports and offered them instead as a consolation to the families of mountain climbing accident victims. Almost forty years later Pfister (1930) presented a psychoanalytic interpretation of dying experiences based largely upon Heim's observations. He felt that they represented a profound regression and denial of death. Hunter (1967), in a recent case report, offered a similar interpretation.

Albert von St. Gallen Heim was especially distinguished for his research on the structure of the Alps and for the light it shed upon the structure of mountain masses in general. He was born in Zurich, April 12, 1849, and attended Zurich and Berlin Universities. Early in life he became interested in the configuration of the Alps and, at the age of sixteen, he made a model of the Tödi group which attracted notice. In 1875 Heim became professor of geology at the University of Zurich, and in 1882 he was appointed director of the geological survey of Switzerland. His magnificent work, *Mechanismus der Gebirgsbildung* (1878) is regarded as a classic. The Wollaston medal was awarded to him in 1904 by the Geological Society of London. He died in 1937 at 88 years of age.

The translation of Heim's article from the German that follows was completed by Roy Kletti. It remains quite close to the original though sentence structure has been altered at points for readability. A single paragraph has been omitted because it departs from the main theme of the article and is not contributory.

REMARKS ON FATAL FALLS, by Albert von St. Gallen Heim

Though I present to the readers of the Yearbook a study of fatal falls in the mountains,

I intend to present neither a series of terrifying stories, describing agonies, nor an enumeration of misfortunes. Let us apply ourselves rather to the scientific study of a horrible event. The subject may thereby lose a portion of its ghastliness. Sometimes, to be sure, a fall is dreadful for the survivors but it is something quite different for the victim himself. I will not speak of the various modes of death through falls in mountains but limit myself to a single point of high interest which is the question: What did the victim experience in the last seconds of his life?

One often has dreadful impressions about this. He thinks of these last seconds as containing extreme desperation, great pain, and fearful anguish, and he seeks to read in the countenances of the disfigured dead signs of anxious distortion. But it is not so! Whether it is a fall from a cliff, a fall from ice or snow, or a fall into a ravine or waterfall is unimportant from this standpoint. The subjective perceptions of those who fall to their deaths are the same whether they fall from the scaffolding of a house or the face of a cliff. It has been proven that one who is run over by a wagon or crushed by a machine, even the drowning person or he who senses himself falling on the battlefield, looks death in the face with similar feelings.

But how are we able to come to this conclusion, since the dead are unable to tell us what they felt? It is because those who have encountered similar misfortunes but escaped death have experienced the same thing. As far as sensation goes, loss of consciousness and death are as one. He who lost consciousness and died could no longer tell us anything; but he who awoke, awoke as though from death and could tell us exactly what those who actually died from sudden misfortune must have experienced. In so doing he will have died twice in his life.

I have drawn the material on which I support my presentation from a variety of sources. Here and there, even if rarely, we find pertinent accounts in the alpine and other literature. In the Hamburg Lazareths of the war year 1870, and on different later occasions, I have questioned those wounded in war. Several physicians who witnessed misfortunes gave me statements about them. I searched out several masons and roofing men who had fallen from scaffolds and roofs in addition to workers who were in disasters in mountain projects and railways. A large number of alpine climbers who had fallen without losing their lives gave me precise information. Men who were thrown off the Elmberg by high gusts of wind and lost consciousness described their experiences to me. Further, I obtained comprehensive reports from fellow club members who had fallen and were rescued as well as from three professional comrades. A fisherman who had nearly drowned described his experiences to me. A good presentation of a close brush with death came from the survivors of the railway disaster on the Mönschenstein. What induced me, however, to accumulate such reports, after I had omitted opportunities for doing so for more than twenty-five years, was my own experience.

In nearly 95 percent of the victims there occurred, independent of the degree of their education, thoroughly similar phenomena, experienced with only slight differences. In practically all individuals who faced death through accidental falls, a similar mental state developed. It represented quite a different state than that experienced in the face of less suddenly occurring mortal dangers. It may be briefly characterized in the following way: no grief was felt, nor was there paralyzing fright of the sort that can happen in instances of lesser danger (e.g. outbreak of fire). There was no anxiety, no trace of despair, no pain; but rather calm seriousness, profound acceptance, and a dominant mental quickness and sense of surety. Mental activity became enormous, rising to a hundred-fold velocity or intensity. The relationships of events and their probable outcomes were overviewed with objective clarity. No confusion entered at all. Time became greatly expanded. The individual acted with lightning-quickness in accord with accurate judgment of his situation. In many cases there followed a sudden review of the individual's entire past; and finally the person falling often heard beautiful music and fell in a superbly blue heaven containing roseate cloudlets. Then consciousness was painlessly extinguished, usually at the moment of impact, and the impact was, at the most, heard but never painfully felt. Apparently hearing is the last of the senses to be extinguished.

Before I turn to several individual accounts, I would like to emphasize two essential points. No pain! Men struck by bullets in wartime all reported to me that they had not felt the entrance of the bullets. They first became aware that they had been hit when a limb no longer moved or when they saw blood flow. Men who had fallen from heights were unaware that their limbs had been broken until they attempted to stand. A 16-year-old Italian boy who had fallen from a scaffold and sustained fractures of his skull and collar bone told me that he had only heard the sound of the bones breaking but had felt no pain at all. He had been able to walk to the hospital by himself. When I myself, as a 16-year-old, was thrown from a wagon drawn by a horse that suddenly became skittish, I could hear cracks and count that I had broken four middle-sized and two small bones. I announced this at once to a doctor who examined me but I could not feel whether the bones had been broken in my legs or my arms, until I saw, as I was picked up, that my left leg and foot were turned backwards and that my knee was bent. Pain was not discernible until some hours later. If a leg or an arm is shattered through a blow from a rock in the mountains, one sees which limb is injured before he feels it. As I fell in the Santis in 1872, I merely heard the blows that injured my head and back; I felt no pain. There are easily a hundred such instances that could be cited, all of which prove that in sudden severe misfortune pain is omitted. This is no doubt a consequence of enormous mental excitement that acts like hypnosis, forcing out sensations of pain with obtruding thoughts. Thus, quite certainly, those who died from falls felt no bodily pain. Paralyzing anxiety was absent, ideational activity seemed enormously increased, and time seemed drawn out. Judgment remained clear and objective, and as far as external circumstances permitted, the faller remained capable of lightning-quick action.

In falls where lifesaving acts are possible, they occur. Of fully thirty examples that have come to my attention I will recall only two. As the weight of three in a band of climbers broke through the ridge on the Piz Palu, Hans Grasz threw himself as a counterweight into the abyss on the other side of the ridge. All in the band remained there, hanging onto the rope joining them over the ridge, and were rescued. As Brantschen, on the Matterhorn in 1877, saw some falling English climbers whose rope, fastened to a crag, hung before him, he bit onto the rope to which they were bound. With both hands he held himself fast to the rope so that he was then able to arrest the plunge of the first of the climbers.

It is not uncommon for children of two years of age or more to save themselves through astonishingly rapid, goal-directed grasps in complicated situations. I have found three remarkable instances of that sort. Surely it is not true to say that such cases show an uncustomary presence of mind simply as a result of surprise. On the contrary, numerous examples prove that the same person who is able to achieve remarkable acts of this sort in the face of death will be completely paralyzed by dread in less dangerous situations. He is no longer able to act so remarkably and is even likely to act in the reverse manner. We conclude that presence of mind arises in response to the highest degree of surprise; in response to a lower degree many persons are, instead, paralyzed.

I maintain that it would also be incorrect were one to satisfy himself with the explanation that such acts merely represent reflex movements. In many acts of this sort automatic defensive movements or involuntary grasping of saving objects do occur. But often falling persons act on the basis of completely conscious, sustained, and complicated series of thoughts that are clear in every respect and often incredibly rapid. In the summer of 1881, I fell between the front and rear wheels of a wagon traveling between Aosta and St. Remy and for a fleeting moment I was still able to hold onto the edge of the wagon. The following series of thoughts went through my mind: "I cannot manage to hold on until the horse comes to a stop; I must let go. If I simply let go, I will fall on my back and the wheel will travel forward over my legs. Then at the least a fracture of the knee-pan or shinbone will be unavoidable; I must fall upon my stomach and the wheel will pass over the backs of my legs. If I will then tense the muscles, they will be a protective cushion for the bones. The pressure of the street will be somewhat less likely to break a bone than the pressure of the wheel. If I am able to turn myself to the left, then perhaps I can sufficiently draw back my left leg; on the other hand, turning to the right would, by the dimensions of the wagon, result in both legs being broken under it." I know quite clearly that I let myself fall only after these lightning-fast, wholly precise reflections, which seemed to imprint themselves upon my brain. Thereupon through a jerk of my arm, I turned myself to the left, swung my left leg powerfully outward, and simultaneously tensed my leg muscles to the limit of their strength. The wheel passed over my right ham, and I came out of it with a slight bruise. Several persons have told me quite similar stories. What they reveal is not merely an admirable presence of mind or a simple reflex movement. Much more than that, they reflect the dread-engendered uttermost exertion of the human spirit appearing in moments of extreme excitement from natural necessity.

A classical presentation of subjective perceptions occurring during sudden accidental falls is contained in the account of a theology student who had fallen with the collapse of the Monschenstein Bridge on June 14, 1891. He shows that the phenomena in different types of misfortunes are essentially similar. I take the following from the "Swiss Protestant Journal" from June 20, 1891:

> The ride was at the fastest possible speed, but very irregular and by fits and starts, so that conversation was impossible. The two locomotives did not work well together, and the rearmost car had to pay for it; for that reason there was no great feeling of security. At first I did not take it seriously when, near the Birs Bridge, I felt a sudden strong shock that ensued from our erratic progress. But at the same moment the train stopped in the middle of the fastest run. The shock threw the riders up to the roof. I sat backwards, unable to see what had happened. From the powerful metallic crashing that resounded up ahead, I presumed there had been a collision. I opened the door and intended to go out. I noticed that the following car had lifted itself upwards and threatened to tumble down on me. I turned in my place and wanted to call to my neighbor at the window: "Out the window!" I closed my mouth as I bit my tongue sharply. Now there took place, in the shortest possible time, the ghastliest descent that one could imagine. I clung spasmodically to my seat. My arms and legs functioned in their usual way, as if instinctively taking care of themselves and, swift as lightning, they made reflex parries of the boards, poles, and benches that were breaking up around and upon me. During this time I had a whole flood of thoughts that went through my brain in the clearest way. The thoughts said, "the next impact will kill me." A series of pictures showed me in rapid succession everything beautiful and lovable that I had ever experienced, and between them sounded the powerful melody of a prelude I had heard in the morning: "God is almighty, Heaven and Earth rest in His hand; we must bow to His will." With this thought in the midst of all the fearful turmoil I was overwhelmed by a feeling of undying peace. Twice more the car swung upwards; then the forward part suddenly headed perpendicularly down into the Birs, and the rear part that I was in swung sideways over

the embankment and down into the Birs. The car was shattered. I lay jammed in and pressed under a heap of boards and benches and expected the next car to come crashing down on my head; but there was sudden quiet. The rumbling noise stopped. Blood dripped from my forehead, but I felt no pain. The loss of blood made me light-headed. After a short struggle I worked my way out of the heaps of fragments and through a window. Just then I formed, for the first time, a conception of the immensity of the disaster that had taken place . . . .

Numerous like-sounding reports have come from people who have suffered falls: A North Böhm postmaster who, in 1871 as an 8-year-old child, fell a full 72 feet off a precipitous cliff reported this to me:

During the fall I experienced absolutely no unpleasant feeling. I clearly recall that I somersaulted in the air three to four times; that made me worry I might lose the pocket knife that my father had given me as a present. In spite of the severe brain-rattling and several skin cuts I got out of it, I can only once again assure you that in the fall itself I had not the slightest unpleasant, painful, or anxious feeling. I did not feel the impact at all since already well before that I had become completely unconscious.

Our club member J. Sigrist, who fell backwards from the peak of the Kärpfstock, reported:

The fall backwards and out was, contrary to what one would think, entirely unaccompanied by the sort of anxious feeling one often has in dreams. Instead, I believed myself to be floating downward in the most pleasant way and I had the fullest consciousness during the fall. Without pain and anxiety I surveyed my situation, the future of my family, and the arrangements I had already made for their security with a rapidity of which I had never before been capable. There was no trace of the loss of breath that people often speak of, and I painlessly lost consciousness only upon the most powerful impact on the cushion of snow covering the crag below. I felt nothing from the cuts I had sustained earlier on my head and limbs. I cannot think of a milder, finer way to die. To be sure, the reawakening brought different sensations.

The verbal accounts of almost all my other informants were quite similar, just as were the stories obtained from Whymper, Tyndall, and others.

In a fall, the moment at which unconsciousness occurs is determined less by the nature of the incident than by the nature of the faller. Alpine climbers who had fallen often told me that while one of their party lost consciousness at the beginning of the fall and knew nothing to report of the rest of it, most of the others first lost consciousness upon violent impact. More frequent were those cases where, without a true loss of consciousness, the faller took corrective action (e.g., after falling into water from a collapsing bridge, wading to shore, and climbing out) without later retaining the slightest recollection of the occurrence or his action. There have also been circumstances in which not only consciousness but also memory was extinguished for a few seconds. During the fall itself the faller, as a rule, remained quiet. A scream was hardly ever heard.

Here I will relate a singular experience of my own during a fall. I can give a complete picture of it of the same sort that has been given me in verbal and written communications from others. I was the head of a skilled band of mountain climbers who, in 1871, were climbing in fairly heavy snow from Blauen Schnee in the Santis down toward the Seealp. We came out above the Fehlalp, about 5,900 feet high on the crooked upper edge of a steep-sided corridor of snow between two of the 240 clearly defined crags of rocks in the Siegfried-Atlas glacial sheet. The others hesitated, but I immediately began leading the way down and our progress went very quickly. Then a draught blew off my hat and instead of letting it go, I impulsively made the mistake of grabbing for it. This movement caused me to fall and to be unable to govern my direction. Propelled by the wind, I dove toward the leftward crag-point, rebounded from the crag-face, sailed back-first and with my head downwards over the crag. At the last I flew freely through the air about 66 feet until I landed on the border of snow under the wall of the crag.

As soon as I began to fall I realized that now I was going to be hurled from the crag and I anticipated the impact that would come. With clawing fingers I dug into the snow in an effort to brake myself. My fingertips were bloody but I felt no pain. I heard clearly the blows on my head and back as they hit each corner of the crag and I heard a dull thud as I struck below. But I first felt pain some hours afterward. The earlier mentioned flood of thoughts began during the fall. What I felt in five to ten seconds could not be described in ten times that length of time. All my thoughts and ideas were coherent and very clear, and in no way susceptible, as are dreams, to obliteration. First of all I took in the possibilities of my fate and said to myself, "the crag point over which I will soon be thrown evidently falls off below me as a steep wall since I have not been able to see the ground at the base of it. It matters a great deal whether or not snow is still lying at the base of the cliff wall. If this is the case, the snow will have melted from the wall and formed a border around the base. If I fall on the border of snow I may come out of this with my life, but if there is no more snow down there, I am certain to fall on rubble and at this velocity death will be quite inevitable. If, when I strike, I am not dead or unconscious I must instantly seize my small flask of spirits of vinegar and put some drops from it on my tongue. I do not want to let go of my alpenstock; perhaps it can still be of use to me." Hence I kept it tightly in my hand. I thought of taking off my glasses and throwing them away so that splinters from them might not injure my eyes, but I was so thrown and swung about that I could not muster the power to move my hands for this purpose. A set of thoughts and ideas then ensued concerning those left behind. I said to myself that upon landing below I ought, indifferent to whether or not I were seriously injured, to immediately call to my companions out of affection for them to say, "I'm all right!" Then my brother and three friends could sufficiently recover from their shock so as to accomplish the fairly difficult descent to me. My next thought was that I would not be able to give my beginning university lecture that had been announced for five days later. I considered how the news of my death would arrive for my loved ones and I consoled them in my thoughts. Then I saw my whole past life take place in many images, as though on a stage at some distance from me. I saw myself as the chief character in the performance. Everything was transfigured as though by a heavenly light and everything was beautiful without grief, without anxiety, and without pain. The memory of very tragic experiences I had had was clear but not saddening. I felt no conflict or strife; conflict had been transmuted into love. Elevated and harmonious thoughts dominated and united the individual images, and like magnificent music a divine calm swept through my soul. I became ever more surrounded by a splendid blue heaven with delicate roseate and violet cloudlets. I swept into it painlessly and softly and I saw that now I was falling freely through the air and that under me a snow field lay waiting. Objective observations, thoughts, and subjective feelings were simultaneous. Then I heard a dull thud and my fall was over.

In moments a black object whisked away from my eyes and I shouted to my companions three to four times, "I'm all right!" I took some of the spirits of vinegar, I grasped my glasses that lay unbroken next to me in the snow, and I felt my back and limbs to confirm that no bones had been broken. Then I saw my companions, who already appeared quite near me, hewing their way slowly step by step to reach me in the corridor of snow beneath the crag-point off which I had flown. I could not understand why they were still so far away. But they told me that for fully a half hour I had made no reply to their calls. It was at this point that I first realized that I had lost consciousness upon impact. The black object had been unconsciousness that evidently had registered in perception a fraction of a second after it had been effected in my brain; and without my observing the interruption, my thoughts and activities had gone on just as they had before. In between there had been subjective absolute nothingness. I experienced the lovely, heavenly representations only as long as I still flew through the air and could see and think. With the loss of consciousness upon impact they, too, were suddenly erased and afterwards no longer continued. After my friend, Andreas Anton Dorig, had set me on my feet I was able to move. Many screams, however, were torn from me by pain in my head and from bruises on my back until, wrapped in ice coverings, I was carried to the Meglisalp. Even so, I gave my beginning lecture at the previously agreed on time.

Quite certainly it is incomparably more painful in both the feeling of the moment and subsequent recollection to see another person fall than to fall oneself. This is attested to by innumerable narratives. Often the spectator, incapacitated by paralyzing horror and quaking in body and soul, carries away from the experience a lasting trauma, while the person whose fall was watched, if he is not badly injured, comes away from his experience free of fright and pain. To be sure there soon follow subsequent reactions of severe headache and immense fatigue. I have seen others fall several times though I have not seen them fall to their deaths. But these memories remain ever dreadful. I must even testify that the memory of a cow's fall is still painful for me while my own misfortune is registered in memory as a pleasant transfiguration—without pain and without anguish—just as it actually had been experienced.

After the newspapers carried some remarks about the report I had given in the Uto Section, I received from Hungary, Bohemia, Germany, and England a large number of letters from persons who had been in climbing accidents. These accounts confirmed the results I had already obtained from numerous earlier ones. Death from falling is horrible only when it is not the quick result of the fall—when the fallen one regains consciousness and then suffers for long hours, days, or even weeks, until he expires.

We have reached the conclusion that death through falling is subjectively a very pleasant death. In the absence of preceding illness it ensues in clear consciousness, in heightened sensory and ideational activity, and without anxiety or pain. Those of our friends who have died in the mountains have, in their last moments, reviewed their individual pasts in states of transfiguration. They have fondly thought of their loved ones. Elevated above corporeal pain, they were under the sway of noble and profound thoughts, heavenly music, and a feeling of peace and reconciliation. They fell in a blue and roseate, magnificent heaven—then everything was suddenly still. Unconsciousness occurred suddenly and without agony; and in this condition a few seconds and a millenium are just as long or just as short. They are a nothingness for us. For those who are unconscious, death can involve no more changing. It is absolute rest. The painless extinguishment remains unaltered.

One might at this point attempt an explanation of these phenomena. But depending upon whether one proceeded from a physiological or from a philosophical standpoint, his explanation might turn out quite variously and lead to quite varied further suppositions. But I will purposely not venture into this insecure province. I wish merely to show the actualities of these enormous elevations of life proffered the human spirit in death through falling, and I would not like to leave the ground of direct observation.

For the survivors, these fatal falls are horrible and cruel. But when I once imparted my conviction and observations about this matter to a mother whose two fine sons had lost their lives in falls, my words were a comfort for her. Then she knew that death for them had been very pleasant. Reconcilement and redeeming peace were the last feelings with which they had taken leave of the world and they had, so to speak, fallen into Heaven.

In spirit, dear comrades, we lay a wreath on the graves of those who have died in falls!

REFERENCES

Bierce, A. An occurrence at Owl Creek Bridge. In W. D. Harells (ed). *The great modern American stories.* New York: Boni & Liveright, 1920, p. 237-247.

Crosby, C. *The passionate years.* New York: Dial Press, 1953, pp. 18-19.

Encyclopedia Britannica, Eleventh Edition, *13,* p. 213.

Heim, A. Notizen über den Tod durch absturz. *Jahrbuch des Schweizer Alpenclub,* 1892, *27,* 327-337.

Hunter, R. C. A. On the experience of nearly dying. *American Journal of Psychiatry,* 1967, *124,* 84-88.

Jaspers, K. *General psychopathology.* Chicago: University of Chicago Press, 1963, pp. 368.

Jung, C. G. *Memories, dreams, reflections.* New York: Pantheon, 1961, pp; 289-298.

Pfister, O. Shockdenken und Shockphantasien bei Hochster todesgefahr. *Zeitschrift fur Psychoanalyse,* 1930, *16,* 430-455.

Poe, E. A. A descent into the Maelstrom. *The complete tales and poems of* . . . New York: Modern Library, 1938, pp. 135.

CHAPTER 14

On Death and the Continuity of Life: A Psychohistorical Perspective[1]

Robert Jay Lifton

Serious concern with the way in which people confront death leads one to question the nature of death and the nature of life in the face of death. In my work in Hiroshima I found that studying an extreme situation such as that facing the survivors of the atomic bomb can lead to insights about everyday death, about ordinary people facing what Kurt Vonnegut has called "plain old death." I feel that our psychological ideas about death have been so stereotyped, so limited, so extraordinarily impoverished, that any exposure to a holocaust like Hiroshima, or My Lai, or in fact the entire American involvement in Indochina, forces us to develop new ideas and hypotheses that begin to account for some of the reactions that we observe. I want to suggest a few such principles that are both psychological and historical.

Technological Violence and Absurd Death

My basic premise is that we understand man through paradigms or models. The choice of the paradigm or model becomes extremely important because it determines what might be called the "controlling image" or central theme of our psychological theory. Human culture is sufficiently rich that a great

[1] An earlier version of this chapter was prepared for the conference on "Death Research: Methods and substance," Berkeley, California, March 21-23, 1973 and also appeared in *The History of Childhood Quarterly*, Spring, 1974, Vol. 1, No. 4, pp. 681-696.

variety of paradigms are available to serve as controlling images, including those of "power," "being," "instinct and defense," "social class," "collective unconscious," "interpersonal relations," etc. These paradigms are by no means of equal merit, but each can be used to illuminate some aspect of human experience.

At the end of my study of Hiroshima, *Death In Life,* I stated that sexuality and moralism had been the central themes confronted by Freud in developing psychoanalysis; but that now unlimited technological violence and absurd death have become more pressing themes for contemporary man [1]. During the Victorian era, when Freud was evolving his ideas, there was an overwhelming repression of sexuality but a relatively greater openness to the reality of human death. The extent of sexual repression is revealed by the Victorian custom of putting doilies on table legs because these were thought to be suggestive of the human anatomy. There has been a historical shift, and the contemporary situation is one in which we are less overwhelmed by sexual difficulties but more overwhelmed by difficulties around death. One can characterize the shift as from covering the legs of tables with doilies to the display of hotpants; and from the grim reaper as public celebrity to the Forest Lawn syndrome. The fact that Freud's model of libido and repression of instinctual sexual impulses was put forth during the late Victorian era, at a time when society was struggling with these issues, does not invalidate the generalizability of his ideas: their power lies precisely in that generalizability. But it does raise the important point—not only for Freud but for our own work now—of the influence of historical forces on the psychological theories we choose to develop. If we now begin to build psychological theory around death it is because death imposes itself upon us in such unmanageable ways.

In my own psychological work on extreme historical situations involving ultimate violence and massive death, I have preferred to speak of a process of psychic numbing rather than repression. Repression occurs when an idea or experience is forgotten, excluded from consciousness, or relegated to the realm of the unconscious. Repressed childhood memories and repressed instinctual impulses are illustrations of this process. Repression is part of a model or controlling image characterized by drives and defenses and refers to the compensatory effort of the organism to cope with innate or instinctual forces that dominate emotional life. The original idea was to analyze these forces and thereby bring the patient to cure.

Psychoanalysis has been changed significantly by the development of ego psychology, by various neo-Freudian modifications, and by many new influences including ethology. But I think that psychoanalytic theory is still bedeviled by its traditional imagery of instinct, repression, and defense. This imagery yields limited and distorted insight when one approaches the subject of death and the relationship of death to larger contemporary experience. The concept of psychic numbing, in contrast, suggests the cessation of what I call the formative process, the impairment of man's essential mental function of symbol-formation or symbolization. This point of view is strongly influenced by the symbolic philosophy of Cassirer and Langer [2]. Psychic numbing is a form of desensitization; it refers to an incapacity to feel or to confront certain kinds of experience, due to the blocking or absence of inner forms or imagery that can connect with such experience.

The importance of this kind of phenomenon was impressed upon me very profoundly by my work in Hiroshima. It would appear that the technology of destruction has had a strong impact on the spread of psychic numbing. But my assumption is that psychic numbing is central in everyday experience as well, and may be identified whenever there is interference in the "formative" mental function, the process of creating viable inner forms. The "psychoformative" perspective would stress that a human being can never simply *receive* a bit of information nakedly. The process of perception is vitally bound up with the process of inner re-creation, in which one utilizes whatever forms are available in individual psychic existence.

Death and the Continuity of Life

SYMBOLIC IMMORTALITY

Within this psychoformative perspective the central paradigm I wish to develop is that of *death and the continuity of life.* In elaborating this paradigm I will speak first of a theory of symbolic immortality, then of an accompanying theory of evolving death imagery, and finally discuss the application of this paradigm in clinical work and psychopathology.

I want to emphasize at the beginning that this approach to psychology and history is impelled by a sense of urgency about our present historical predicament, and by a strong desire to evolve psychohistorical theory adequate to the dangerous times in which we live. In this approach it is necessary to make our own subjectivity as investigators clear and conscious, to try to understand it and use it as part of the conceptual process. I have elsewhere suggested possibilities for going even further and making our forms of advocacy clear, forthright and, again, part of the conceptual process [3]. In presenting this paradigm of death and the continuity of life I also assume a sense of urgency in our intellectual and professional lives. A crisis exists in the psychiatric profession, and in other professions as well, that has to do with despair about the adequacy of traditional ideas for coping with new data impinging from all sides.

In his book *The Structure of Scientific Revolutions* [4] Thomas Kuhn describes a sequence that occurs in the development of scientific thought when the data can no longer be explained by prevailing theories. Kuhn observed that when this happens the usual reaction among scientists is to cling to the old theories all the more persistently. At a certain point the incongruity between the theory and data becomes so glaring—and the anxiety of those defending the theory so great—that the whole system collapses and the paradigm changes. I think we are at a point something like that now, and that a new depth-psychological paradigm is required. Ironically, the paradigm of death and the continuity of life is actually man's oldest and most fundamental paradigm.

Psychiatrists and psychoanalysts have for the most part left the question of death to philosophers. Freud's theory legitimized this neglect when he said:

> It is indeed impossible to imagine our own death: and whenever we attempt to do so we can perceive that we are in fact still present as spectators. Hence the psychoanalytic school could venture on the assertion that at bottom no one believes in his own death, or, to put the same thing in another way, that in his unconscious, every one of us is convinced of his own immortality [5].

Freud viewed all interest in immortality as compensatory, as a denial of death and a refusal to face it unflinchingly. Freud insisted that we look at death squarely, that we cannot psychologically afford the consequences of denial. But Freud had no place in his system for the *symbolic* significance of the idea of immortality as an expression of continuity. For this reason I call Freud's approach "rationalist-iconoclastic."

Jung's approach was very different; he took the mythological and symbolic aspects of death and immortality very seriously. He emphasized the enormous significance of the idea of immortality on the basis of the map of the human psyche, and especially of the unconscious, provided by mythology. But he also said: "As a physician I am convinced that it is hygenic to discover in death a goal toward which one can strive: and that shrinking away from it is something unhealthy and abnormal": and, "I . . . consider the religious teaching of a life hereafter consonant with the standpoint of psychic hygiene" [6]. In such statements it becomes unclear whether Jung is talking about the literal idea of a life after death or a more symbolic one. He surrenders much of the scientific viewpoint, however broadly defined, that man has struggled for so painfully over the last few centuries. We can thus call Jung's approach "hygienic-mythical."

Both of these views are important: neither is completely satisfactory. Freud's attitude has the merit of unflinching acceptance of death as a total annihilation of the organism. Jung's view has the merit of stressing the symbolic significance of universal imagery around death and immortality.

A third perspective—which I shall call "formative-symbolic"—draws upon both Freud and Jung but takes into account the increasing awareness of symbol-formation as a fundamental characteristic of man's psychic life. I should emphasize that I am speaking of an on-going *process of symbolization,* rather than of particular symbols (the flag, the cross, etc.). In classical psycho-analysis the focus tends to be in symbols as specific equivalents—pencil for penis, sea for mother, etc.—and much less upon the more fundamental process of creation and re-creation of images and forms that characterize human mentation.

I would hold, in the context of this psychoformative view, that even in our unconscious lives we are by no means *convinced* of our own immortality. Rather we have what some recent workers have called "middle knowledge" [7] of the idea of death. We both "know" that we will die, and resist and fail to act upon that knowledge. Nor is the need to transcend death *mere* denial. More essentially, it represents a compelling universal urge to maintain an inner sense of continuous symbolic relationship, over time and space, with the various elements of life. In other words, I am speaking of a *sense* of immortality as in itself neither compensatory nor pathological, but as man's symbolization of his ties with both his biological fellows and his history, past and future. This view is consistent with Otto Rank's stress on man's perpetual need for "an assurance of eternal survival for his self." Rank suggested that "man creates culture by changing natural conditions in order to maintain his spiritual self" [8]. But this need for a sense of symbolic immortality, inter-woven with man's biology and his history, is for the most part ignored by individually-biased psychological theory.

The sense of immortality can be expressed in five general modes. The first and most obvious is the biological mode, the sense of living on *through* and *in* one's sons and daughters and their sons and daughters. At some level of con-sciousness we imagine an endless chain of biological attachments. This mode has been a classical expression of symbolic immortality in East Asian culture, especially in traditional China, with its extraordinary emphasis on the family line. In Confucian ethics, the greatest of all unfilial acts is lack of posterity. But this mode never remains purely biological: it becomes simultaneously biosocial, and expresses itself in attachments to one's group, tribe, organiza-tion, people, nation or even species. Ultimately one can feel at least glimmerings of a sense of immortality in "living on" through and in mankind.

A second expression of the sense of immortality is the theological idea of a life after death or, more importantly, the idea of release from profane life to existence on a higher plane. The literal idea of an afterlife is not essential to this mode and such a notion is not present in many religions. More basic is the concept of transcending death through spiritual attainment. The power of spiritual life to in some way overcome death is exemplified in all the great religious leaders around whom religions have been founded: Buddha, Moses, Christ, Mohammed. Within each of the religious traditions there has been a word to convey the spiritual state in which one has transcended death: the Japanese word *kami*; the Polynesian term *mana*; the Roman idea of *noumen*; the Eskimo concept of *tungnik* and the Christian doctrine of *grace*. All these words describe a state in which one possesses spiritual power over death, meaning, in a symbolic sense, that one is in harmony with a principle extending beyond the limited biological life span.

The third mode of symbolic immortality is that achieved through "works": the mode of creativity, the achievement of enduring human impact; the sense that one's writing, one's teaching, one's human influences, great or humble, will live on; that one's contribution will not die. The therapeutic efforts of physicians and psychotherapists are strongly impelled, I believe, by an image of therapeutic impact extending through the patient to others, including the patient's children, in an endless potentially beneficient chain of influence. The "therapeutic despair" described so sensitively by Leslie Farber [9] as an occupational hazard of the psychiatrist treating schizophrenic patients might well result from the perception that one's strenuous therapeutic endeavors are not producing these lasting effects, that one's energies are not animating the life of the patient and can not therefore symbolically extend the life of the therapist.

A fourth mode is the sense of immortality achieved through being survived by nature itself: the theme of eternal nature. This theme is very vivid among the Japanese, and was one of the most important kinds of imagery for survivors of the atomic bomb. It is strong not only in Shinto belief, but in the European Romantic movement and in the Anglo-Saxon cult of the great outdoors—indeed in every culture in one form or another.

The fifth mode is somewhat different from the others in that it depends solely upon a psychic state. This is the state of "experiential transcendence," a state so intense that in it time and death disappear. When one achieves ecstasy or rapture, the restrictions of the senses—including the sense of mortality—no longer exist. Poetically and religiously this has been described as "losing oneself." It can occur not only in religious or secular mysticism, but also in song, dance, battle, sexual love, childbirth, athletic effort, mechanical flight, or in contemplating works of artistic or intellectual creation [10]. This state is characterized by extraordinary psychic unity and perceptual intensity. But there also occurs, as we hear described in drug experiences, a process of symbolic reordering. One feels oneself to be different after returning from this state. I see experiential transcendence and its aftermath as epitomizing the death-and-rebirth experience. It is central to change or transformation and has great significance for psychotherapy. Experiential transcendence includes a feeling of what Eliade has called "continuous present" that can be equated with eternity or with "mythical time" [11]. This continuous present is perceived as not only "here and now" but as inseparable from past and future.

The theory of symbolic immortality can be used to illuminate changes in cultural emphasis from one historical period to another. We can think of historical shifts as involving alterations in the stress given to one or another mode or combinations of modes. The Darwinian revolution of the 19th century, for example, can be seen as entailing a shift from a predominantly theological mode to a more natural and biological one. The continuous transformation in China over the last few decades involves a shift from a family-centered biological mode to a revolutionary mode, which I have written about elsewhere as emphasizing man's works but as including also elements of other modes with periodic emphasis upon experiential transcendence [12].

Following the holocaust of World War II the viability of psychic activity within the modes has undergone something of a collapse, at least in the West. We exist now in a time of doubt about modes of continuity and connection, and I believe this has direct relevance for work with individual patients. Awareness of our historical predicament—of threats posed by nuclear weapons, environmental destruction, and the press of rising population against limited resources—has created extensive imagery of extinction. These threats occur at a time when the rate of historical velocity and the resulting psychohistorical dislocation had already undermined established symbols around the institutions of family, church, government, and education. Combined imagery of extinction and dislocation leave us in doubt about whether we will "live on" in our children and their children, in our groups and organizations, in our works, in our spirituality, or even in nature, which we now know to be vulnerable to our pollutions and our weaponry. It is the loss of faith, I think, in these four modes of symbolic immortality that leads people, especially the young, to plunge—sometimes desperately and sometimes with considerable self-realization—into the mode of experiential transcendence. This very old and classical form of personal quest has had to be discovered anew in the face of doubts about the other four modes.

REPRESENTATIONS OF DEATH

In postulating a theory of symbolic immortality on such a grand scale, one must also account for the everyday idea of death, for the sense of *mortality* that develops over the course of a lifetime. Freud's notion of the death instinct is unacceptable, could in fact be viewed as a contradiction in terms in that instinctual forces are in the service of the preservation of life. Nor is death an adequate goal for life. Yet as is generally the case with Freud when we disagree with him, the concept, whatever its confusions around the instinctual idiom, contains an insight we had best retain concerning the fundamental importance of death for psychological life. Hence, the widespread re-

jection of the death instinct poses the danger not so much of throwing out
the baby with the bath water but perhaps the grim reaper with the scythe.

Freud himself faced death heroically and understood well the dangers involved in denying man's mortality. But at the same time Freudian theory,
insisting that death has no representation in the unconscious, has relegated fear
of death to a derivative of fear of castration. Freud also seemed ambivalent
about whether to view death and life within a unitary or dualistic perspective.
His ultimate instinctual dualism opposed death and life instincts. Yet the
notion of life leading inevitably toward death is a unitary vision, and it is
this unitary element that I think we should preserve. This unitary perspective
on death would insist upon its overall consistency as an absolute infringe-
ment upon the organism (as opposed to certain contemporary efforts to
subdivide death into a number of different categories); and as an event
anticipated, and therefore influential, from the beginning of the life of the
organism.

I believe that the representation of death evolves from dim and vague
articulation in the young organism's inchoate imagery to sophisticated symbolization in maturity. I rely partly here on Kenneth Boulding's work on the
image [13], in which he has stressed the presence in the organism from the
very beginning of some innate tendency or direction which I call an *inchoate
image.* This image is at first simply a direction or physiological "push." But
inchoate though it may be, the image includes an *interpretative anticipation
of interaction with the environment.* Evidence for the existence of innate
imagery can be drawn from two sources; one is ethology and the other is
observation of rapid eyeball movements (REM) in sleep studies.

Work in ethology has demonstrated through the study of "releasing
mechanisms" the existence of what I am here calling an image. The newborn
organism is impelled innately toward certain expected behavior on the part
of older (nurturing) organisms, which when encountered, acts as a releasing
mechanism for a specific action (such as feeding) of its own. Sleep studies
also suggest the presence of images in some form from the beginning of life,
possibly during prenatal experience, that "cause" or at least provide some
basis for the rapid eyeball movements observed in various species. Rather than
demonstrating the presence of pictorial images, these two areas of research
suggest the presence at birth of primordial images or precursors to later
imagery.

In the human being the sequence of this process is from physiological
push (or direction of the organism), to pictures of the world (images in the
usual sense) to symbolization. Within this theory of evolving imagery we can
understand the elaboration of the inner idea of death from earliest childhood
in terms of three subparadigms or polarities. These are: connection versus

separation, integrity versus disintegration, and movement versus stasis. The inchoate imagery of the first polarity is expressed in a seeking of connection, what John Bowlby has described as "attachment behavior" around sucking, clinging, smiling, crying and following [14]. The organism actively seeks connection with the nurturing or mothering person. First this quest is mainly physiological, then is internalized in pictorial image-formation, and finally becomes highly symbolized. The organism's evolution is from simple movement toward the mother to a nurturing relationship with her, and eventually toward connection with other people, with groups, with ideas, with historical forces, etc. Where this striving for connection fails, as it always must in some degree, there is the alternative image of separation, of being cut off. This alternative image of separation forms one precursor for the idea of death.

In a similar way one can look at the idea of integrity versus disintegration. As indicated in the work of Melanie Klein on the infant's fear of annihilation [15], there is from the beginning some sense of the organism's being threatened with dissolution, disintegration. The terms of this negative image or fear are at first entirely physiological, having to do with physical intactness or deterioration; but over the course of time integrity, without entirely losing its physiological reference, comes to assume primarily ethical-psychological dimensions. At those more symbolized dimensions one "disintegrates" as one's inner forms and images become inadequate representations of the self-world relationship and inadequate bases for action.

The third mode, that of movement versus statis, is the most ignored of the three; but it has great clinical significance and is especially vivid to those who deal with children. An infant held tight and unable to move becomes extremely anxious and uncomfortable. The early meaning of movement is the literal, physiological idea of moving the body or a portion of it from one place to another. Later the meaning of movement takes on symbolic qualities having to do with development, progress and change (or with a specific collectivity in some form of motion). The absence of movement becomes a form of stasis, a deathlike experience closely related to psychic numbing.

One could illustrate in detail the evolution of these polarities over the course of the life cycle. But it is clear that rather early, or earlier than is usually assumed, death achieves some kind of conscious meaning. By the age of three, four, and five children are thinking and talking, however confusedly, about death and dying. And over the course of the next few years something in that process consolidates so that the idea of death is more fundamentally learned and understood. At every developmental level all conflicts exacerbate, and are exacerbated by, these three aspects of what later becomes death anxiety—that is, disintegration, stasis or separation. These death-linked conflicts take on characteristic form for each developmental stage and reach a climax during adolescence. During young adulthood there occurs a process partly described by Kenneth Kenistion around the term "youth" [16], and partly described in my own work around the concept of the "Protean style" [17]. I see the continuing search characterizing the Protean style as a constant process of death and rebirth of inner form. The quest is always for images and forms more malleable and inwardly acceptable at this historical moment than are those available from the past. Sometime in early adulthood one moves more fully into the realm of historical action and one then connects with the modes of symbolic immortality.

Later, in middle adulthood, one becomes impressed that one will indeed die. It becomes apparent that the limitations of physiology and life span will not permit the full accomplishment of all one's projects. But even with this fuller recognition of mortality the issues of integrity, connection and movement remain salient. Old people approaching death look back nostalgically over their whole lives. This "life review" as it is sometimes called, has to do with a process of self-judgment, of examining one's life around issues of integrity, but also of connection and movement; and for evidence of relationship to the modes of symbolic immortality.

CLINICAL APPLICATIONS

How do these principles apply in mental disturbance? I want to suggest the clinical applicability of this paradigm of death and the continuity of life for various categories of psychopathology. Psychiatrists have turned away from death, as has our whole culture, and there has been little appreciation of the importance of death anxiety in the precipitation of psychological disorder.

What I am here calling the sense of immortality is close to what Erik Erikson calls basic trust [18]. Erikson emphasizes the issue of basic trust as the earliest developmental crisis and he sees the legacy of this earliest time as having vital importance for adulthood. But the establishment of trust itself involves confidence in the integrity, connection and movement of life, prerequisites for a viable form of symbolic immortality. Where this confidence collapses psychological impairment ensues.

The principle of impaired death imagery—or more accurately, of impaired imagery of death and the continuity of life—is a unitary theme around which mental illness can be described and in some degree understood. I see this kind of impairment as being involved in the etiology of mental illness but not as causative in the nineteenth century sense of a single cause bringing about one specific effect. Rather, impaired death imagery is at the center of a constellation of forms, each of which is of some importance for the overall process we call mental disturbance. Here I would point to three relevant issues central to the process of mental illness. The first is death anxiety;

which evolves in relation to the three polarities I have described. The second is psychic numbing, which I see as a process of desymbolization and deformation. The image which accompanies psychic numbing is that "if I feel nothing then death does not exist; therefore I need not feel anxious about death either actually or symbolically; I am invulnerable." A third principle is what I call "suspicion of counterfeit nurturance." This is the idea that if death exists then life is counterfeit. Ionesco's question—Why was I born if it wasn't forever?—illustrates the relation of this theme to the quest for immortality. But it is a very old question.

Death anxiety can be seen as a signal of threat to the organism, threat now understood as disintegration, stasis or separation. All anxiety relates to these equivalents of death imagery, and guilt too is generated insofar as one makes oneself "responsible" for these processes. In other writings I have distinguished between static (either numbed or self-lacerating) and animating guilt, and have emphasized the importance of the latter in the process of self-transformation [19].

One can take as a model for much of neurosis the syndrome which used to be called "traumatic neurosis" or "war neurosis." It is generally described as involving the continuous re-living of the unconscious conflicts aroused by the traumatic situation. More recently emphasis has been placed on imagery of death aroused by the trauma, rather than the trauma *per se.* Thus the syndrome has been called by some observers "death anxiety neurosis" [20]. I see this process in terms of the psychology of the survivor as I have elaborated that psychology in my work on Hiroshima and more recently with antiwar veterans. My belief is that survivor conflicts emerge from and apply to everyday psychological experience as well. When one "outlives" something or someone, and there are of course many large and small survivals in anyone's life, the specter of premature death becomes vivid. Simultaneously one begins to feel what I came to call in my Hiroshima work "guilt over survival priority"— the notion that one's life was purchased at the cost of another's, that one was able to survive *because* someone else died. This is a classical survivor process and is very much involved in traumatic neurosis. In describing traumatic neurosis, earlier observers spoke of "ego contraction" [21]. This is close to what I call psychic numbing, also very marked in the survivor syndrome and in neurosis in general.

A great number of writers (including Stekel, Rank, Horney, and Tillich) have emphasized patterns closely resembling psychic numbing as the essence of neurosis. Stekel, in 1908, spoke of neurotics who "die every day" and who "play the game of dying" [22]. Otto Rank referred to the neurotic's "constant restriction of life" because "he refuses the loan (life) in order to avoid the payment of the debt (death)" [23]. The neurotic thus seeks to defend himself against stimuli in a way Freud described in a little-known passage in *Civilization and Its Discontents.* Freud observed:

No matter how much we may shrink with horror from certain situations—of a galley slave in antiquity, of a peasant during the Thirty Years War, of a victim of the Holy Inquisition, of a Jew awaiting a pogrom — it is nevertheless impossible for us to feel our way into such people, to divine the changes which original obtuseness of mind, a gradual stupifying process, the cessation of expectations and cruder of more refined methods of narcotization have produced upon their receptivity to sensations of pleasure and unpleasure. Moreover, in the case of the most extreme possibility of suffering, special mental protective devices are brought into operation [24].

It is strange that Freud turned away from his own argument at this point and concluded that it was "unprofitable to pursue this aspect of the problem any further." For that argument contained the core of the idea of psychic numbing in extreme situations. The holocausts described by Freud have become almost a norm, a model for our times. But in lesser degree, what Freud called narcotization and I am calling psychic numbing is associated with the individual "holocausts" and survivals around which neurosis takes shape.

Let me now make some preliminary suggestions about the significance of these struggles around death imagery for the classical psychiatric syndromes. I am exploring these relationships more fully in work in progress [25], and my hope is that others will as well.

If we view neurosis in general as an expression of psychic numbing— shrinking of the ego and diminished capacity for experience—we can see in depression specific examples of impaired mourning, impaired symbolization, and the impaired formulation of the survivor. Where a known loss triggers the process, as in reactive depression, the depressed person acts very much like a survivor and psychic numbing becomes very prominent. He often expresses the feeling that a part of him has died, and that he "killed" the other person in some symbolic way by failing to sustain the other's life with needed support, help and nurturance. The idea of either having killed the other person or of having purchased one's own life at the cost of another person's is fundamental. Such feelings are also related to Freud's explanation of guilt, in that earlier ambivalent feelings toward the other person included hate and death wishes, which now become attached to the actual loss. The whole issue of grief and its relation to mental disturbance is too complex to examine fully here. I can only say here that grief is of enormous importance in the experience of survival and in its residuum of mental and physical disturbance related to psychic numbing.

In character disorders, and in the related phenomenon of psychosomatic disorders in which one speaks through the "language of the body," there are lifelong characterological patterns of deadening or numbing of various aspects of the psyche. This numbing may involve moral sensitivity or interpersonal capacities. However the numbing is expressed, there is a situation of meaninglessness and unfulfilled life, in which the defensive psychological structures built up to ward off death anxiety also ward off autonomy and self-under-standing.

Turning to hysteria, the "psychic anesthesia" emphasized in early litera-ture suggests the centrality of stasis, deadening, or numbing. Freud's case of Anna O., for example, is properly understood as a mourning reaction [26]. The hysteria followed very quickly upon the death of Anna's father and had much to do with her reaction to that death. Her conception of being alive became altered in such a way that merely to *live* and *feel*—to exist as a sexual being—was dangerous, impermissable, and a violation of an unspoken pact with the dead person. Whether or not there is a mourning reaction directly involved, hysteria tends to involve either this form of stasis or its seeming opposite, exaggerated movement or activity that serves as a similar barrier against feeling and living. These patterns again resemble those I encountered among Hiroshima survivors.

In obsessional neurosis and obsessive-compulsive styles of behavior the stress is upon order and control. One tries to "stop time," to control its flow so as to order existence and block spontaneous expression, which is in turn felt to be threatening and "deadly."

Much of Freudian theory of phobia evolved from the case of Little Hans. In this case Freud interpreted castration fears as being displaced and trans-formed into a fear of horses—the inner danger being transformed into an ex-ternal one [27]. But I would say that Little Hans' experience could also be understood in terms of fear of annihilation and separation. His castration fear epitomized but was not the cause of his general death anxiety. Rather than viewing this death anxiety as secondary to castration anxiety, as psychoanalytic literature has done ever since, we do better to reverse our understanding and interpret the castration anxiety as an expression of more general death anxiety.

Finally I want to turn to psychosis and to an application of this theoreti-cal position to schizophrenia. One is appalled by the degree to which death imagery has been observed in schizophrenic persons without being really incorporated into any conceptual scheme. As with more general psychiatric concern with death, the situation is changing. Harold Searles writes at some length about the problems a schizophrenic person has with the "universal factor of mortality." Searles says that the schizophrenic patient doesn't really believe he is living, doesn't feel himself to be alive, feels life passing him by, and feels stalked by death. Thus the patient employs a variety of techniques to defend himself against death anxiety, and yet in another sense feels him-self already dead, "having therefore nothing to lose through death" [28]. And what Ronald Laing calls the "false self" is very close to what I am calling a numbed or "dead self." Laing goes on to "translate" from what he calls "schizophrenese" and describes "the desire to be dead, the desire for a

non-being" as "perhaps the most dangerous desire that can be pursued"; and
the "state of death-in-life" as both a response to "the primary guilt of having
no right to life in the first place, and hence of being entitled at most only to
a dead life" and "probably the most extreme defensive posture that can be
adopted" in which "being dead, one cannot die, and one cannot kill" [29].
What Searles and Laing describe in schizophrenics is directly reminiscent of
the process I observed among survivors in Hiroshima, and is similar to the
Musselmanner phenomenon that occurred in Nazi concentration camps: so
extreme was the state of psychic numbing that, as one observer put it, "One
hesitates to call their death death" [30]. These were people who had become
robots.

The schizophrenic experiences a pathetic illusion of omnipotence, a
despairing mask of pseudo-immortality because he is blocked in the most
fundamental way from authentic connection or continuity—from what I have
been calling a sense of symbolic immortality.

But the productions of the schizophrenic are infused with death: again
like the Hiroshima survivors at the time the bomb fell, he sees himself as
dead, other people around him as dead, the world as dead.

Wynne, Lidz, and others who have studied family process in schizophrenia
emphasize the transmission of "meaninglessness, pointlessness, and emptiness,"
of "irrationality," of "schism and skew" [31]. Bateson's "double bind"
theory of conflicted messages received by the child also stresses the difficulty
faced by the child in establishing a coherent field of meaning [32]. All of
these theories represent a transmission of "desymbolized" or "deformed"
images, which cannot cohere for the child and which leave him overwhelmed
with death anxiety and suspicion of counterfeit nurturance. In the child's
experience nurturance is dangerous: he flees from it into isolation, stasis, a
"safer death" of his own.

It may require several generations to produce a schizophrenic person. But
one can say that, however the inheritance mechanism may operate, whatever the contribution of genetic legacy, the early life of the schizophrenic is
flooded with death anxiety, and the result is thought disorder and impairment
of reality sense. The schizophrenic's behavior and symptoms represent alternate tendencies of surrender to death anxiety and struggle against it. The
near total suspicion of counterfeit nurturance which characterizes the
schizophrenic's emotional life renders his psychic numbing more extensive and
more enduring than in any other form of psychiatric disturbance. Although
one sometimes sees in acute forms of schizophrenia an exaggerated response
to stimuli, the general and long-range process is one of profound psychic
numbing. To the schizophrenic as to certain survivors of mass holocausts, life
is counterfeit, inner death predominant, and biological death unacceptable.
Because the schizophrenic's entire existence has been a series of unabsorbable

death immersions and survivals, he ultimately settles for a "devil's bargain": a lifeless life.

The paradigm of death and continuity of life I have elaborated here—together with psychoformative and psychohistorical perspectives—can help keep psychiatry and psychoanalysis close to their biological origins without imposing on them an instinctual determinism. The paradigm recognizes the scope of man's symbolization and provides a link between his biology and his history, a link essential to make if either is to be sustained.

I close with a few quotations. The first is a slogan from an eighteenth century guild—very simply: "Remember to die." Ostensibly it was a reminder to make advance funeral arrangements through the guild, but, however inadvertently, it conveys much more. The next is from the playwrite Peter Weiss, who said, "Once we thought a few hundred corpses would be enough, then we said thousands were still too few; today we can't even count all the corpses everywhere you look." Finally, Yeats:

Man is in love and loves what vanishes, What more is there to say?

REFERENCES

1. Robert Jay Lifton, *Death in Life*, New York: Random House, 1968, pp. 540-541.
2. See Ernst Cassier, *An Essay on May*, Doubleday Anchor, 1944, *The Myth of the State*, Doubleday Anchor, 1946, and *The Philosophy of Symbolic Forms* (three volumes), New Haven: Yale Univ. Press, 1953-1957; and Susanne Langer, *Philosophy in a New Key*, Cambridge: Harvard Univ. Press, 1942, *Feeling and Form*, New York: Scribners, 1953, *Philosophical Sketches*, Baltimore: Johns Hopkins Press, 1962, and *Mind: An Essay on Feeling*, Baltimore, Johns Hopkins Press, 1967.
3. Lifton, "Experiments in Advocacy Research," *Research and Relevance*, Vol. XXI of Science and Psychoanalysis, ed. J. H. Masserman, pp. 259-271. Also in the academy newsletter of The American Academy of Psychoanalysis, Feb. 1972, Vol. 16, No. 1, pp. 8-13.
4. Thomas Kuhn, *The Structure of Scientific Revolutions*, Chicago: Univ. of Chicago Press, Phoenix Books, 1962.
5. Sigmund Freud, "Thoughts for the Times on War and Death," Standard Edition, London: The Holgarth Press and the Institute of Psychoanalysis, 1957, Vol. XIV, p. 289.
6. Carl Jung, *Modern Man in Search of a Soul*, New York: Harcourt Brace, 1936, p. 129.
7. Avery Weisman and Thomas Hackett, "Predilection to Death: Death and Dying as a Psychiatric Problem," *Psychosomatic Medicine*, May-June 1961, Vol. 33, No. 3.
8. Otto Rank, *Beyond Psychology*, New York: Dover reprint, 1958, p. 64.

9. Leslie Farber, "The Therapeutic Despair," *The Ways of the Will*, New York/London: Basic Books (2nd printing), 1966.

10. Marghanita Laski, *Ecstasy: A Study of Some Secular and Religious Experiences*, Bloomington: Indiana Univ. Press, 1961.

11. Marcea Eliade, *Cosmos and History: The Myth of the Eternal Return*, New York: Harper Torchbacks, 1959.

12. Lifton, *Revolutionary Immortality: Mao Tse-tung and the Chinese Revolution*, New York: Random House, 1968, p. 10.

13. Kenneth Boulding, *The Image*, Ann Arbor: Univ. of Michigan Press, 1956.

14. John Bowlby, *Attachment and Loss* (Vol. I: Attachment), New York: Basic Books, 1969.

15. Melanie Klein, et al, *Developments in Psychoanalysis*, London: The Hogarth Press, 1952.

16. Kenneth Keniston, *Young Radicals*, New York: Harcourt, Brace and & Jovanovich, 1968.

17. Lifton, "Protean Man," *Partisan Review*, Winter 1968, Vol. 35, 1:13-27; *History and Human Survival*, New York: Random House, 1970, pp. 311-331; and *Archives of General Psychiatry*, April 1971, 24:298-304.

18. Erik H. Erikson, *Childhood and Society*, New York: Norton, 1950.

19. Lifton, *Home From the War: Vietnam Veterans, Neither Victims Nor Executioners*, New York: Simon & Schuster, 1973.

20. Joseph D. Teicher, " 'Combat Fatigue' or 'Death Anxiety Neurosis'," *Journal of Nervous and Mental Disease*, 1953, 117:234-242.

21. Abram Kardiner, "Traumatic Neuroses of War," *American Handbook of Psychiatry*, 1959, Vol. I, pp. 246-257.

22. Wilhelm Stekel, *Nervous Anxiety States and Their Treatment* (translated by Rosalie Gabler), New York: Dodd Mead & Co., 1923, as cited in Jacques

23. Rank, *Will Therapy*, New York: Knopf, 1950.

24. Freud, *Civilization and Its Discontents*, Standard Edition, Vol. XXI, p. 89.

25. Lifton, *The Broken Connection*, ms., chapter on "Death and Psychiatry."

26. George R. Krupp and Bernard Kligfeld, "The Bereavement Reaction: A Cross Cultural Evaluation," *Journal of Religion and Health*, I, 1962, pp. 222-246.

27. Freud, "Analysis of a Phobia in a Five-Year-Old Boy," Standard Edition, Vol. X, pp. 5-149.

28. Harold Searles, "Schizophrenia and the Inevitability of Death," *Psychiatric Quarterly*, 1961, 35:631-635.

29. R. D. Laing, *The Divided Self*, Baltimore: Penguin (Pelican), 1965, p. 176.

30. Primo Levi, *Survival In Auschwitz*, New York: Collier, 1961, p. 82.

31. See, for instance, various papers in Don B. Jackson (ed.), *The Etiology of Schizophrenia*, New York: Basic Books, 1960.

32. Ibid.

CHAPTER
15

The Coffin

J. H.

PROLOGUE — DEATH

Now it was over. The big job. The one I had worked so hard to get. I knew I had done it well, but time had run out on me and now it was over. So what? Or rather, now what? Anything from here on would be anti-climax. Today I was a somebody; tomorrow a nobody. What price mediocrity?

I stared at the ceiling. The door. The wall. The ventilator grill. The ventilator grill? I had wondered about it before. Now I studied it seriously. Was it high enough? Could I shove something through the latticework? Would it support my weight? And if all these factors were favorable (or unfavorable — depending on the point of view), would I have guts enough to go through with it? I decided to find out.

THE COFFIN — LIMBO

After my clothes had been removed, they opened the coffin and put me inside. Then they shut the coffin and went away. I lay there a long time trying to figure out what had happened before I realized I was dead. Having never died before, I didn't know what it would be like. I didn't know the rules. I got the feeling that I might have to create my own rules of unexistence — sort of play it by ear.

Then I began to take stock of my surroundings. It was a large coffin with nothing in it. Nothing, that is, except a wash basin, a commode, two windows, and a corpse. I thought about the wash basin. Do dead people wash? Unlikely. I would not use it. The commode. Do dead people excrete? Probably not, but I decided I would use it if I had to. The windows. A small one to be looked in; a large one to be looked out. Did I dare to look out their in-window? Did they dare to look in my out-window? There was no hurry. I would find out later when I got used to being dead.

The coffin was opened. There were three of them. One of them threw in a pallet, another a covering. The third one stared at my body, still and pale in death. They closed the coffin and went away. Do dead people use pallets? Of course. I placed my corpse on the pallet. And the covering? Yes. Keep the body warm.

153

I lay there a long time. I tried to figure out why I was dead. Had I died a natural death? Not likely. Had they killed me? That didn't seem to be the answer either. Had I killed myself? Probably. But why? I couldn't remember.

Then I began to wonder how long I would be dead. How long is long when you're dead? There is no way to measure time spent in death. There is no yesterday, no today, no tomorrow. There is only the forever of the moment, the infinity of the now.

So I lay there a long time and then the coffin opened again and they gave me a tray of food, closed the coffin, and went away. I looked at the food. Do dead people eat? No. I would not eat. Days passed and they came again and took the tray away.

Again I tried not to think, but another question posed itself. Can dead people think? Probably not. I would stop thinking.

And so the days passed into weeks and the weeks into months. Once I looked out the in-window and saw one of them looking at me, so I didn't do it again.

And the months passed into years and the years into decades and they left the trays and took them away again. And then one day the coffin opened and with them stood the Creator. I felt the breath of his life flowing toward me and breaking my rules of death I dared to speak. "May I be born again?" His voice, rising from the depths of eternity, answered, "You have not yet earned the right to be born again." So they closed the coffin and went away. And I returned to the frustration, the agony, the hopeless limbo of my unlife.

And the decades passed into centuries and the centuries into eons and then one day someone looked in my out-window. It was a friend from countless ages in the past and his unspoken thoughts seeped into my dead mind, "Why did you do it? Why? Why? We all needed you so much." And I started to weep, but then I remembered that the dead don't cry and I tried to check myself, but couldn't hold it back. "To hell with the rules," I thought, and wept unashamedly.

And as I wept, the coffin opened and the Creator spoke to me in a gentle voice. "You may have your life back. Use it more wisely than you did before. Come out. You are born again."

EPILOGUE — BIRTH

I stood in the hall in my underwear, looking and feeling rather foolish. A friend came up and spoke to me. "Man, you sure look rocky. Anything I can do for you?" "Yeah, Dunc buddy," I answered, putting my hand on his shoulder. "You can score a couple of smokes for us. Then you can help me celebrate my rebirth."

He reached in his pocket, pulled out a cigarette, and lit it for me. Looking at me quizzically, he spoke again. "That sure was a goofy thing you did. You could have died, you know." "I did, buddy," I said, thinking over the last six days, "that's just exactly what I did."